The New Brand You

Your New Image Makes the Sale for You

ISBN 9780991906024

Copy Editing by: Cathy Reed
Cover Design by: Darko Knezevik
Text and Layout by: Iryna Spica

Printed and Bound in the USA

The New Brand You

Your New Image Makes the Sale for You

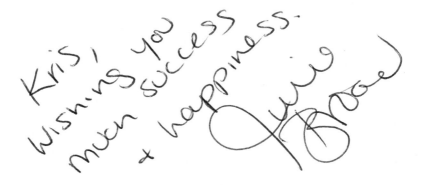

Kris,
wishing you
much success
+ happiness.
Julie Broad

By Julie Broad

STICK HORSE PUBLISHING

2016

To Dave – everything is better with you by my side.
I love you.

Table of Contents

Introduction

Standing in front of a whiteboard in a small, brightly lit meeting room, 12 people faced me, waiting. Tears filled my eyes. My hands were sweaty and shaking.

I was trying to think of something to draw. The only rule was that it couldn't be anything related to real estate.

I had an MBA in real estate and finance. I'd been investing for ten years, and teaching people how to invest for three years. My husband was my business partner. *Everything in my life* – including a great number of my friends – was real estate related.

I couldn't think of a single thing I would do if it wasn't real estate related.

A door was opening in front of my mind, but it was pitch black inside that room.

I was terrified to go inside; any number of scary things could be waiting for me.

Yet I still felt a magnetic pull to that room.

What if it wasn't bad at all? I was *almost* as curious as I was afraid. But I was too fearful to take that step.

Would *you* step into the pitch black room?

The people in the room were watching, supporting me to enter that room, but I was defiant.

I declared that I was already doing exactly what I wanted to do – writing and teaching.

When I left that day, I went back to doing what I knew, but that door didn't close.

When I wasn't busy working on our real estate deals, or teaching people how to invest in their own real estate deals, that dark room haunted me. The open door called to me.

The fears and possibilities chased me like ghosts. I'd worked hard to create the life I was living, and it was pretty darn good. I dreaded the effort that it might take to start something new. And I worried that it wouldn't be as fun, or that I wouldn't be good enough or strong enough to do whatever it was that I wanted to do next. But the feeling that so much more was possible would not go away.

The question 'Was it possible there was life after real estate?' was changing to 'What will my life beyond real estate be?'

But, before I get into that, let's talk about you.

WHAT DO YOU REALLY WANT TO DO?

The question is not: "What can you make money doing?"

The question is: "What do you really want to do?"

Not what you think is possible, but what you want to do.

As I started searching for what else I wanted to do, I wasn't the only one in our house thinking about what else was possible besides real estate. My husband (and business partner for more than a decade) Dave was exploring acting, and he had become quite serious about making a career of it.

As he found himself trying to manage our existing portfolio, speaking with our coaching clients, and building an acting career, he realized something had to go. He was being pulled in too many different directions to do a good job of anything.

It was time for change. Gulp....

There's a reason we fear change. It's hard. It's emotional. It's uncomfortable.

The worst part can be figuring out the first step. And then the next step.

If you're about to venture into something new, you already know this. You have a level of comfort in what you do today. You may not enjoy it, or want to do it forever, but there's comfort because you know what to expect.

But change can also be exhilarating and full of possibility.

Whether you're changing careers, or going from student to employee, employee to entrepreneur, or entrepreneur in one type of business to entrepreneur in another, you have to reinvent yourself.

You have to showcase expertise you haven't emphasized before, because you have been doing something different.

How do you influence others to see you in the way you want them to see you? How do you positively impact those around you? And how do you make an income doing it?

By creating your personal brand.

Creating a great brand – one that reflects clearly who you are and what you do – makes everything easier. And the *stronger* your brand, the more money you will be paid.

You have a brand already.

We all have a brand, but few of us have taken time to cultivate it and become comfortable with selling ourselves within that brand. We let things happen to us instead of getting in the driver's seat and *making* things happen.

You can let people come up with their own idea of who you are and what value you bring to the world, and then hope they see you the way you'd like to be seen. Or, *you can consciously create and shape your brand and communicate it to others.*

You don't need to reach millions of people to have a powerful impact and earn a great living. But you do need to know how to communicate and present who you are and what you do. You *do* need a personal brand that connects with the right people.

That is what this book is going to help you with.

It will provide you with a solid foundation to help you become known as an expert or an authority in your industry, and you will feel more comfortable selling yourself in that role. You may even be making more money doing what you do before you're finished reading this book.

WHY THIS BOOK?

Building a strong brand is the single most powerful way to get your dream job, uncover cool opportunities, or start/grow a business. When most people think about branding they think about colors, logos, and websites. That's *corporate* branding. That's not *personal* branding.

Your brand is YOU.

It's your character. It's your values. It's how other people see you. It's your story and how you communicate your message.

How do you build the brand that is *YOU*?

That's what this book is about. Yes, we'll touch on logos, social media, websites, etc., but none of that matters if you aren't clear on who *you* are, and how *you* want to connect with others.

There are other books on branding, of course, but most are written from a *corporate* perspective. There are a few well known personal branding books, like the one by Tom Peters, and the more recent one by Dorie Clark. Their insights are excellent for helping you build a personal brand to switch jobs or climb the corporate ladder, but what about when you change career paths *entirely*? Research by Workopolis shows that three-quarters of us will change career paths entirely at least twice in our lifetime.[1] And, what if you're amongst the growing population of people who are more focused on creating your own business or a specific lifestyle than making your way up the corporate ladder? If that's you, the existing books don't really address what's most important for you.

I've also found that many books on personal branding are difficult to relate to. They are either highly technical (send 100 Tweets a day, post four photos on Instagram, and here's how to understand Facebook's algorithm to get more Likes); or they are from the perspective of a celebrity like the Kardashians or Trump. Trying to learn how to brand yourself by looking at what celebrities have done is a bit like watching *Lifestyles of the Rich and Famous* when you live in a rented one-bedroom apartment. It may be cool to look into someone else's world, but none of it feels like it applies to *you*.

This book is about *you* taking action and applying what you read. It's ideal for you if you want a brand that supports you living a specific lifestyle, or if you want to start or grow a business where *you* are the featured expert. It's carefully researched, tested and written so that *you* can apply what you learn, no matter what your business goal is. It's not about covering the technical details; it's about covering the practical ones. Most of the technical things like 'how do I set up a website on WordPress' or 'how do I create my LinkedIn Profile,' you can find by searching on Google. This book covers the things you need to know that *aren't* found on Google.

WHAT TO EXPECT FROM THIS BOOK

Implementing *one powerful idea* today can impact you in all kinds of ways for years to come. The idea that I should get my money *working* for me came from a book I read in the year 2000.[2] Implementing that

---

1   http://careers.workopolis.com/advice/how-many-jobs-do-canadians-hold-in-a-lifetime/

2   Robert Kiyosaki, *Rich Dad Poor Dad* (New York: Warner Books, 1997).

idea not only made me a lot of money; it also opened my mind and my life to so many other opportunities and people! The book wasn't the only thing, and the implementation didn't happen overnight, but it was the beginning of something important and powerful for me.

I hope that this book you are now reading can be a cool new beginning for you, or a critical step on your journey.

This book isn't written to impress you; if you read about an achievement of mine, it's because there's a lesson to be learned from it. I've heard it said this way: "This story is not to impress you, but to impress *upon* you..."

You'll read about my mistakes because you'll benefit from knowing where I went wrong.

You need the truth. I promise to do my best to openly share my truth with you, so you have the full story to make your own choices for your life and your brand.

You need to know that it takes work. Sometimes it takes *a lot* of work. And it takes time; but if you're doing the *right* work, it will feel important, and it will even feel fun, and you'll *want* to put time into it.

This book is not a marketing piece for me. In fact, when you read how hard it is to build a great brand you may not want to do it. You may let the chips fall where they may and just hope that things work out.

There's no *upsell*. The only offer you'll find inside these pages is to connect with me online at *www.HaveMoreInfluence.com* so I can keep sharing tips, tools and stories with you through my (almost) weekly *Broad Thoughts Newsletter*. To make that connection easy, there's a QR Code in the back of this book...or you can just visit the website.

You have the power to positively impact people all around you. *You can create a great life doing something that matters to you.* And, you don't have to feel ready to do it; you don't have to feel comfortable or confident yet; you just have to start and take the first step into *that dark room*.

This book is about making that change to create a great life for you and your family *and* it's about having a great impact on those around you.

So are you ready to finally help the people you know you were meant to help – to help them land that promotion, pay raise, revenue boost or dream job? Are you ready for people to know who you are and what you offer?

You're about to learn:

- How to get people to listen to you and care about what you have to say

- Why Jamie Fox changed his name to be gender neutral

- An exercise to help you get clear on what you want your personal brand to be

- The Magic Brand Formula to create an authentically YOU brand

- The five key stories you need to tell, and how to tell them for maximum impact

- About the time I forgot to put my pants on

- Why hiring a ghostwriter might be the way to create your brand

- How you can build a great brand, even if you're a wallflower or an introvert

- That you are who Google says you are, so how do you handle that?

THE MISSING PIECE FOR YOUR SUCCESS

If you've been to a motivational seminar, you probably left jacked up and ready to write a best seller, double your income, or save the world.

You go home with the best of intentions but then you find your child has the flu, there's a crisis at work, or you just don't know where to start! It's like Mike Tyson said: *"Everyone has a plan until they get punched in the mouth."*

Suddenly weeks pass after the event, and you're just not sure if your idea is that great after all. Or even if you still think it's a great idea, and you want to do it, a voice in your head kicks in and says, *"Okay, sure that sounds great, but how do I actually do it?"*

That's when I get excited. Yes, I enjoy a good dose of inspiration and motivation, but my favorite thing is creating a clear action plan and getting to work.

The quote I've been saying for years is: *"The missing piece is <u>always</u> action."*

Get excited about creating your action plan. Get pumped about taking action, and look forward to seeing results, fast.

I think (I hope!) you're going to love what's ahead, so let's get into it....

CHAPTER 1

When Selling Scares the Pants Off You!

It was February 2000. I had just been promoted from a sales rep to an account manager, and it was an hour before my first big head office sales presentation.

I worked for Kimberly Clark Canada selling Kleenex, Kotex and Huggies, and like many sales reps in the packaged goods industry, I worked from home.

I was prepping to leave when my phone rang. *"Julie, just wanted to check in and see if you're ready? Do you have the samples?"*

My manager wanted to make sure I was all set for the meeting.

I chatted with her for about 10 minutes, reviewing the details of my presentation, and then I had to rush. I checked that I had everything I needed for the presentation – samples, slide deck, car keys....

I had butterflies in my stomach so I took a deep breath as I closed my apartment door, locked it, and walked down the hallway toward the stairwell. I got to the door, opened it, and felt a rush of air on my legs.

Too much air...

I looked down ... I wasn't wearing any pants!

With all the excitement and nerves around this first meeting, I had been totally distracted and hadn't finished getting dressed! I rushed back to my apartment, unlocked the door and found my pants.

Selling can be nerve wracking; it certainly didn't feel comfortable or come naturally to me. As a sales rep going store-to-store selling Kleenex, Huggies and Kotex, I had more than one sales call that ended with me in my car crying. The buyers were scary and I hated the feeling I got when I tried to convince someone to do something. I dreaded when I had to ask someone for more promotional display space or extra signage; I always got so tense and tongue-tied.

If you feel uncomfortable pitching your idea or selling yourself, I get it. The thought of building a personal brand and shining a spotlight on yourself might even make you feel shaky.

It's scary to put yourself out there where people can judge you, reject you, and otherwise make you feel terrible. And all those things you're afraid of probably will happen in some form.

Sorry, you were probably looking for reassurance, yes? But you need to know that on occasion you will be judged, so mentally prepare for it.

People will post things online that they would never say to your face – mean and even totally false things. You will be rejected. Your service, product, or idea is not for everyone. And some people will criticize you only because they are jealous or frustrated that you're doing something they want to do.

It sucks when it happens, but we'll talk about why those people aren't worth your attention, and who to focus on instead.

MY GREATEST FEAR AS AN AUTHOR HAPPENED

"Very disappointed – No real practical advice"

Amazon.ca reviewer of *More Than Cashflow*

It took me a few years to write and publish my first book. The actual process of going from draft to published book took time, but the biggest hold-up was coming from me. I had this deep fear that people would hate my book.

These are my words, my stories, my thoughts. By hating my book, it feels, in a weird way, like you hate me. I may never have met you, but I want you to like me. I want you to feel like I've delivered massive value to you and your life.

I wrote that in present tense on purpose. I'm much more comfortable with who I am today and what I can do for others, yet I still feel that way. I still fear you won't like me or find value in these pages.

I've accepted that this fear will probably never go away. I just try to recognize when it might be holding me back so I can work with it and move forward anyway.

If you want to have an impact on others, you must stand out. But when you stand out you will be judged, and that can be terrifying.

Public speaking is one of the greatest fears. People aren't afraid of opening their mouth and letting words come out; most do that quite easily - some maybe too easily.

A fear of public speaking isn't a fear about speaking; it's a fear of being *judged* by the people in the audience.

But here's what you need to know...

The people who will judge and criticize you are NOT the ones achieving greatness, creating success and having a lasting positive impact on others. *Those* people are way too busy to criticize you. They know how hard it is to put yourself out there, so they aren't about to judge you for doing it, even if you could do it better. Also, *most people do want you to succeed* and will support you.

Think about it for a second. Did you pick up this book hoping it would be a terrible and useless read? Likely you wanted me to succeed in writing a useful, inspiring, entertaining book, right? It's the same when you sit down to hear a speaker – you want them to be fun, engaging and educational, right?

Your audience wants you to succeed.

> *You can't let the voice of one person who is miserable in their life ruin the positive message that the majority of people are giving you.*

Yes, I felt hurt when I saw the one-star Amazon review. I was even mad.

Then I wondered what kind of book he was looking for if he felt mine was not practical. I knew my book was *very* practical.

After a few moments, I moved on.

The solution to most challenges is almost always that you have to do the very thing you're afraid of doing.

So face your fear … yes, the worst *might* happen, but more likely it will leave you laughing that you were ever afraid of that one-star review.

OPEN YOUR EYES TO THE OPPORTUNITIES

Fifty percent of sales situations fail because the sales person never *asked* for the sale.[1]

I bet the number is even higher than that when you factor in how many people never even realize they are in a potential sales situation.

> *It's time to open your eyes to what you want, what you offer and who you are best suited to help.*

Once you realize the gift you have to share with others, why not shout it from the rooftops?

---

1   Jeffrey Gitomer said this at Influence Bootcamp in 2015. The stat is based on his experience.

Marie Forleo published an excellent video in June 2015 where she talked about how we like to announce we're going to promote ourselves by saying this is 'shameless self promotion.' She said, *"Instead of calling it shameless self-promotion, let's take the shame out of it altogether."*[2]

The most interesting thing about people is usually their achievements ... the things they have accomplished against the odds. Yet, think about what you talk about when you meet someone new. It's usually what you do for a living, where you live and if you have kids.

There is an art to *sharing* your accomplishments and what you do that's cool, so that people will connect with you and want to know more. There is a difference between sharing and bragging.

We'll be covering the soft sell approach to subtly promoting what you do and attracting the best people and opportunities. You don't need to be in someone's face with what you do – you can do it in a comfortable and conversational way. Let me explain.

HOW TO INCREASE YOUR SALES BY 386% WITH A SOFT SELL

"So you're painting your house? Did you consider Hardie Plank Siding?"

My husband and I were standing on the sidewalk, staring up at our home as we chatted with the guy who was going to install new windows for us. The task ahead was daunting – renovating the exterior of our early 1900's character home.

The conversation carried on for less than 10 minutes. At the end, this fellow who had been hired to install new windows took the $7,000 window job and turned it into a $27,000 job that included replacing all our wood panels with Hardie Plank Siding.

He wasn't a salesperson; he was a tradesperson running a small business. He was the guy who hauled the materials, did the work, and

---

2   http://www.marieforleo.com/2015/07/promote-proudly/

got really dirty doing it. He had one guy helping him full time and another that came on board for bigger jobs.

But he did what so few people do well. He saw an opportunity and he:

- Understood the process perfectly (he had a high level of expertise);

- Asked great questions to understand our situation;

- Proposed a solution that gave us what we really wanted; and

- Didn't worry about what the other guys were offering – his focus was solely on what we needed.

It's not about win-win. I dislike that phrase (sorry, Stephen Covey). I think win-win still puts the focus on *winning*. It still creates an air of competition and control, and it also creates a fear of potential loss.

Selling is about finding solutions that help people.

It requires a number of elements to be in place, but once you have that, people will be stepping forward asking to work with you, offering the very thing you want them to do/say/buy, and it will seem almost magical.

In this case, it was a short conversation but there was a lot that happened for Gary (the window guy) to almost quadruple his business in 10 minutes. We'll cover that later....

First, I want to focus on *how* he was able to turn the $7,000 sale into a $27,000 sale, because this is probably the most important thing you can do right now in your life and business to start increasing your *impact and influence.*

OPEN YOUR EYES TO OPPORTUNITY

My guess is that almost every day you're missing opportunities to have a bigger impact, boost your business, create the life you want, and positively influence those around you *because* you aren't tuned into the opportunities that are right in front of you. And, the worst part is that your customer or client would probably be *so much happier* if you did help them even more.

I was at a private clinic saying goodbye to my underarm hair with laser hair removal (sorry – I know this is probably way more information than you wanted, but stick with me). In the treatment room there were posters on the wall for different treatments – everything from wrinkle reduction to achieving a more even skin color.

I said to the woman that runs the clinic, *"I was just looking at your posters. Looks like I have a few other things to cover. Maybe poster 4 next?"*

She looked over at poster 4 and said, "Yes, collagen can be a good thing to start addressing in your 30's."

It was a perfect opportunity for her to say, "What concerns you most about your skin?" or, "What would you like to change?" She didn't though; she actually switched the conversation back to something unrelated.

I went back four times to finish my original treatment. I never talked about the other treatments again and neither did she. Possibly she didn't want to seem pushy, but my guess is she didn't see the opportunity at all.

This entire book could be filled with examples like this where individuals or businesses have opportunities right in front of them to add a new client or serve their current clients better, and they miss out.

Imagine there's a pile of cash on the ground in front of you. Instead of stopping to investigate whether it could be yours, you keep walking. That's what you're doing if you're not paying attention.

When you're shopping, or hiring service professionals, watch for the missed opportunities. *They are everywhere.*

Imagine you're buying a coffee at your local coffee shop as the cinnamon buns come out of the oven. They smell delicious. You may not ask for one, but a simple "Would you like a warm cinnamon bun with your coffee?" might be an invitation you can't resist.

When you're buying a new sweater and the salesperson picks out the perfect scarf to go with it, you might be delighted to add it to your purchase.

When you order a meal, does the server suggest something else to go with it – a new wine or their signature salad?

Notice that in these examples, you wouldn't feel imposed upon; you would feel well served!

The opportunities to make people happy, give them what they want, and make money doing it are probably right in front of you. As you begin to see these opportunities in other people's businesses, you'll hopefully start to see them in your own as well.

FINDING YOUR IDEAL – A QUICK EXERCISE

It's impossible to find what you want if you aren't sure *what* you're looking for or *why*.

 Think about what your ideal typical day looks like. I'm not talking about a day at the beach where you sip fruity cocktails reading a great book. I'm talking about a day that you live over and over again. What do you do to generate an income, to create whatever it is you're driven to create? What makes you feel fulfilled and gives your life meaning? Who do you spend time with? What do you eat? When do you exercise or take care of yourself?

This is important because a clear vision of what you want your life to look like makes decision-making easier and more efficient. All you have to do is ask yourself: "Does this move me closer to my ideal day, or not?"

Years ago, my husband and I learned an exercise from Michael Losier, author of a book called *Law of Attraction: The Science of Attracting More of What You Want and Less of What You Don't*. We told him that the common challenges we faced in raising money to buy real estate were:

1) we'd find people with money but it wasn't enough money for one deal; or 2) we'd find people with a lot of money but they weren't sure if they wanted to invest in *real estate*.

Losier's exercise helps you to identify your ideal, whatever it is....

We wanted to identify our *ideal investor*.

It's often easier to consider what you *don't* want than to figure out what you *do* want, so Michael suggested we use this exercise:

What I Don't Want	What I Do Want

Go ahead, pull out your pen, and write in the book if you want to! Or go to TheNewBrandYou.com and download the worksheets.

Here's what to do:

Start with writing down what you *don't* want. Make a big list. Outline everything you don't want in your ideal <blank>. This works for a job, a project, a date, a client, an employee, a business, a home, etc. Listing what you *don't* want is actually pretty easy.

When we did this exercise, we noted things we *didn't* want in an investor:

- Wants to be actively involved in day-to-day decisions about the property

- Not enough capital to fully fund a deal

- Wants a quick return on their money and needs the capital back soon

- Worries about a lot of different potential problems

- Is a close friend or family member.

Once you have the list of things you *don't* want, it's much easier to identify what you *do* want.

By doing this exercise, we learned that we wanted an investor who:

- Wanted to invest in real estate but not do any of the work

- Had the financial capability to do multiple deals (for our goals this meant the person had access to at least $200,000 in investable capital)

- Was happy to invest the money for at least five years

- Was eager to let us make most of the decisions because they trusted our expertise

- Was outside our immediate social circle.

From there we were able to visualize what our ideal investor did for a living, whether they had invested in real estate before, what other assets they had invested in, and what kind of relationship we would have with them.

Once you're that specific, it is easy to spot an opportunity. Your ideal person will never walk out of your store, office, or meeting without you at least identifying that there's a *potential* opportunity there.

SELLING HAIR GROWTH SOLUTIONS TO BALD MEN

Just because you're selling a product to help hair grow back doesn't mean every bald man is your ideal client.

My Dad just turned 70; he's been married 40 years; and he's bald. He's been bald a long time and he is totally fine with it. He's not going to spend a penny on a hair growth product.

Just because you have a great solution doesn't mean everybody with that problem will spend money on your solution.

It might feel like you're reducing your potential prospects, but it really means you're perfectly positioning yourself to attract the exact right people for your service. You're also going to save your time and energy for the people who really want your help.

My Dad will probably listen to what you have to say about making his hair grow back. He's retired. He spends his mornings walking around the mall in Nanaimo chatting with a lot of people, but you're not going to get him to open his wallet. Dad wants to keep his head from getting sunburned but that's it.

So, who are you looking for? Again, use the above exercise to help you figure it out. Maybe it would look something like this:

What I Don't Want	What I Do Want
Men who don't care about their appearance	Men who recognize that their appearance impacts their income and their influence, and who invest in staying in shape and dressing well.
Men with full heads of hair	Men with thinning hair or receding hairlines
Men who don't have money to spend on discretionary things like hair care	Men with disposable income
Happily married men and men who are fine with being bald	Single or divorced men who want to impress and attract women

By creating a more specific list of what you want, you begin to form a picture of who you're looking for. You'll begin to see them everywhere you go. So, while it may seem limiting at first, it actually makes the person you're looking for easier to spot.

Whether you're trying to find a new job, selling a product or service, or looking to hire someone to work with you, getting crystal clear on exactly what you're looking for is the most critical step you can take. Once you know how to spot and connect with your ideal person, the entire process gets easier.

 KEY ACTION STEPS:

- People will judge you. Try not to focus on them. Turn your attention to those that you can help and impact.

- Open your eyes to opportunity – it's often right in front of you.

- What is your ideal day that you want to create?

- Identify the ideals for your business and your brand: what is that person, job, or opportunity you are looking for right now? Get crystal clear on what you're looking for.

- Check that you're wearing pants before you leave the house.

CHAPTER 2

Grandma Broad's Words of Wisdom

I was working at my desk when the phone rang. It was my Mom. *"Your Grandma isn't doing well. They rushed her to the ER last night. She has a blockage and needs surgery."*

Surgery is risky at any age. When you're 97, the risks skyrocket.

I immediately booked flights for us to go to see her.

Grandmas are special, and my Grandma Broad is extra special to me.

Grandma always shares words of wisdom. These aren't quotes from other people; her words are the very principles by which she lives.

When I say, *"Have a great day, Grandma,"* she often responds by saying, *"Well dear, it's my own fault if I don't."*

When she was in the hospital, her situation was critical. We were all so worried, but she wasn't.

She stated emphatically, *"I need the surgery. This is no way to live."* If she was worried about surviving the surgery, she never showed it. As we all looked on with worry and concern, she looked back calmly and confidently.

Even the surgeon was thrilled with how well she recovered from surgery. Not only did she survive; she left intensive care and went back home within a week. The only evidence of what had happened was a portable oxygen tank, which she did not like at all. Grandma was used to being very mobile and it was slowing her down.

At her age, once you're on oxygen, it's tough to get off. Most people resolve themselves to that fate, but not Grandma Broad.

The doctors said if she could build up her lung capacity, she wouldn't need the oxygen. They gave her a plastic contraption to breathe into every 30 minutes when she was awake to help build up her lungs.

Even though it made her light-headed, she was blowing into it every 30 minutes on the dot. In less than a month she was off the oxygen and free to walk around the building and go to exercise class again. She proudly shares that she's the only one in the Chair Aerobics class that doesn't really need to be sitting for the class.

Grandma accepts what she can't control and changes what she can. She makes it a great day, whatever the situation.

WHO INSPIRES YOU?

 Take a moment to think about it. Write the name(s) here, or on the worksheets you can download from TheNewBrandYou.com.

For me, my Grandma Broad is at the top of that list. But what is it about *her* that makes her so inspirational?

When I'm faced with a challenge or something that scares me, I think of what she would do or say. I consider how she handles life with such grace and gratitude, and it always helps me through tough moments.

Why do certain people in your life inspire you, while others don't?

The Oxford Dictionary defines "inspiration" as *"The process of being mentally stimulated to do or feel something, especially to do something creative."*

When you jump off the couch to go for a run, or you sit down at your computer to write, there's usually something that made you choose that over something easier. Maybe you've hired a fitness coach and you hear their voice telling you to get at it. Possibly your wife has stepped into a new, gratifying role at work and you feel inspired to achieve something great in your business as well.

WHO IS SITTING AT YOUR TABLE?

It's 1930. You're sitting at a table in a darkly lit pub called the *Eagle and Child* in Oxford with a few friends.

One of your friends clears his throat to address the group. He picks up a page from a stack of papers in front of him and says, "I'd like to read the first line from the book I am working on."

> *"In a hole in the ground there lived a hobbit. Not a nasty, dirty, wet hole, filled with the ends of worms and an oozy smell, nor yet a dry, bare, sandy hole with nothing in it to sit down on or to eat: it was a hobbit-hole, and that means comfort."*

He looks up and waits for the others at the table to comment.

Maybe he knew it at the time, or maybe he didn't, but as J.R. Tolkien worked on *The Hobbit,* he had surrounded himself with some of the greatest literary minds in England at that time.

Every week, C.S. Lewis and J.R. Tolkien gathered a small group of fellow Oxford men, jokingly calling themselves the *'Inklings,'* for readings and criticism of their work and for general conversation. *The Hobbit* and, later, *The Lord of the Rings* were born during the 1930's and 1940's when the Inklings were meeting.

Other well-known works to come from the members of the Inklings during those decades included:

- Charles Williams' *Descent into Hell* and *All Hallow's Eve*

- C.S. Lewis' "Space Trilogy" – *Out of the Silent Planet, Perelandra, That Hideous Strength,* and then the *Chronicles of Narnia.*

In reading about the Inklings,[3] you'll find more than a dozen names associated with the group over the time they met. All were very accomplished, most were Oxford instructors, and almost all were published.

Is it as simple as like attracts like?

Naturally that is part of it. We like people who are similar to us – whether it's similar in opinion, personality traits, lifestyle or background.[4]

But, I think the bigger part of this story is that Tolkien and Lewis *set up* the group to meet for the purpose of making friends and improving their work.

They consciously chose to invite and connect with people who challenged them, supported them, and made them better.

Who is in your life right now that pushes you to be better? Who in your life says '*Was that your best?*' Who in your life cheers (and means it) when you achieve?

The principle of surrounding yourself with the right people is not new. Napoleon Hill's book *Think and Grow Rich* cited this as a success secret of the uber-successful in his day, including Ford, Schwab, Wrigley and many others who are household names even now, 80 years later.

---

3 Wikipedia: http://tolkiengateway.net/wiki/Inklings and http://www.mythsoc. org/inklings/; Carole and Philip Zaleski, *The Fellowship: The Literary Lives of the Inklings: J.R.R. Tolkien, C. S. Lewis, Owen Barfield, Charles Williams.*

4 Robert B. Cialdini, *Influence: The Psychology of Persuasion*, (New York: Collins, 2007), 173.

In his book, he states that the first step to turning your desire into action is to:

> *Ally yourself with a group of as many people as you may need for the creation and carrying out of your plan or plans for the accumulation of money – making use of the "Master Mind" principle described in a later chapter. Compliance with this instruction is absolutely essential. Do not neglect it.*

Maybe you're lucky enough to already be friends with a brilliant mind like C.S. Lewis and other folks who are supporting you and encouraging you; but in case you're not, focusing on finding people who can support you and encourage you (and you'll do the same for them) is really important.

HOW TO GET SIX-PACK ABS

A few years ago, my husband Dave wanted to get six-pack abs for his 40th birthday.

While always active and athletic, Dave also loves food. He's the kind of guy who puts a cookie on top of a donut because he loves treats so much. When he set out to get in the best shape of his adult life, it took a lot of discipline, and the biggest change for him was kicking sugar to the curb.

At first everyone was so supportive; they cheered for him and congratulated him for setting his goal.

But as he lost weight and started to get leaner, people started to change. At a barbecue, a friend was insistent Dave drink a beer, even after he'd already declined. *"One beer isn't going to change whether you get a six-pack, Dave!"* he said as he shoved the beer in front of Dave's face.

At a birthday party, a close family member put a piece of cake in front of him after he'd already said no thanks.

If I had pointed out how unsupportive they were being, they probably would have felt horrible. I doubt they were conscious of what they were doing.

As you set out to create your brand and build a business around it, you will find that some of the people closest to you will try to hold you back from changing or standing out from the crowd. It might come in the form of pressure to take a weekend off when you've planned to spend the weekend researching your competitors. It might appear as encouragement to loosen up and have more beers at the pub even though your friends know you have an important meeting the next day. And it absolutely will come in the form of comments like: *"You work too hard!"* and *"Why would you ever want to do that?"*

If you're not satisfied with your fitness level, the money you make, or your attitude – the most powerful thing you can do is *change who you hang out with*.

In 2012, I realized I wasn't happy with my fitness level anymore. I was still working out, but I felt myself getting soft and out of shape.

I joined Crossfit Nanaimo. It's not just a gym, it's a community of people who cheer for you and challenge you. Before working out there, I couldn't do a single pull-up, and while I could jog 5 km, I was slow and it was usually uncomfortable. Now it's tough, but I can do 50 pull-ups in a workout. And my goal of running 10 km in 50 minutes is within reach.

Yes, I've been working hard, but the big results are because I have great people like Coach Katie and my workout partner Breanne cheering me on every single day.

When I decided to leave my job and become an entrepreneur in 2008, I'd been reading a daily newsletter put out by Michael Masterson. I flew to Florida to learn how to start a business online from his company, invested $3,000 USD to join a group called the Internet Money Club, and connected with other people who were building businesses online.

It worked. We launched our online education business and I left my job to grow it. Each of the first four years, we grew the revenue by 50 to 100 percent.

When we wanted to grow our real estate business from doing 3 to 5 deals a year to doing 10 to 12 deals, my husband Dave hired a mentor named Greg Habstritt and joined a Mastermind group run by Greg. We quickly figured out what we needed to improve in our business, and we started raising millions in investment capital to grow our business and our portfolio, adding 10 houses a year and eventually adding commercial real estate as well.

Many people from both groups are some of the most successful people in their industry today. *It's not a coincidence.* Look back at C.S. Lewis. There is a direct correlation between people who invest in surrounding themselves with people who will push them to achieve success and support them in their aspirations.

You need people around you who will lift you up as they climb. And, you need people around you that you can lift up as you climb.

We found that just about every big achievement in our lives followed that formula … *get stuck, hire help, find a few like-minded achievers to associate with, and then work toward that massive growth spurt.*

You probably already have a friend or two that is fully supporting you. Maybe you just haven't paid close enough attention to the attitudes and actions of those around you. Now that you understand the importance of surrounding yourself with the right people, observe those around you to find the gems you probably already have in your life.

You need to pay attention to the messages coming from your friends and choose your friends wisely. But it's worth noting that your happiness, fitness level and success are more complex than just one close friend helping you to reach your goals (or sabotaging them).

According to research from Nicholas A. Christakis and James Fowler, **if you have a happy friend within one mile, there's a 25% chance you'll become happy too.**

They conclude: *"Happiness is thus not merely a function of individual experience or choice; it's also **a property of groups of people**.*[5]"

They also looked at obesity. It was a complex and lengthy study – covering 32 years of research. It turns out that **obesity is contagious**. We naturally imitate those around us and fall in line with social norms. If people around you are getting fit, then you'll probably get fit. If they are getting fat, you're probably going to gain pounds too.

You probably already know that it's important to choose who you spend your time with, but did you realize that *their* choice of companions impacts you too?

 Take a moment … consider who you are currently spending time with. Does their attitude inspire you? Do the messages you hear from them support your dreams and challenge you to be your best?

Do your friends reflect some of the key elements and characteristics that you want others to associate with *you*?

If you're answering *no*, then perhaps you need to make some changes. If you think you do, write one specific thing you're going to change regarding who you're hanging out with – so it will help you grow.

OUR BEHAVIORS SPREAD LIKE GERMS

It can be a little unsettling to accept the fact that your entire life can be so dramatically impacted by the people you are around, but here's the part that gets me excited:

---

5   Nicholas A. Christakis and James H. Fowler, *Connected: How Your Friends' Friends' Friends Affect Everything You Feel, Think, and Do*, (New York: Back Bay Books, 2009), 54.

Your potential impact is so much greater than you realize.

How you choose to carry yourself and take care of yourself defines your brand. It will also impact your immediate friends, their friends, and even further, their friends. **People you haven't even met yet will be positively impacted by what you do!**

When you take better care of yourself, others will do the same. Similarly, your random acts of kindness will spread. And when you challenge yourself, others will try something new too.

My Grandma has inspired me to handle life's curve balls with more grace. *I don't always have a choice about what happens in my life, but I do always have a choice regarding how I react.*

To take a page from my Grandma's book of life – "make it a great day" – and watch those around you do the same!

 KEY ACTION ITEMS:

- Who inspires you, and why?

- Who do you spend most of your time with? Are those people pushing you to be your best, or are they holding you back? What changes are you going to make?

- Accept what you cannot change, and act on what you can change.

CHAPTER 3

What's Your Big Idea?

"My company also handles quality testing for Voice over IP (VoIP) for small to medium-sized businesses."

I was at a local networking event for the Chamber of Commerce chatting with one of the members I had just met.

I have a full-time assistant in India. She's been working with me for over three years and one of her primary jobs has always been to handle my phone calls. Nobody is going to dial an international number, so we set up a local number on an internet phone. Unless we tell people she isn't in Canada, very few people know. In fact when I told one long-time client where she lived, he was stunned. He said, *"You've just blown my mind! I always pictured her sitting beside you in the office and now you're telling me she doesn't even live in Canada."*

So most people have no idea, but sometimes the connection can be terrible. It sounds like someone on a cell phone with bad service.

I was interested in how I could improve the quality and consistency of calls and work with a local company to do it.

"Have you helped anyone get it set up for a team in India or the Philippines?" I asked him.

He ignored the specificity of my question and went on to excitedly explain how he has office numbers in three cities, all local to each city, and they just route to him in his Nanaimo office. *"Nobody ever knows I'm not in their city when they call,"* he giggled.

I tried again. *"What carrier do you use so the quality is high enough that people don't realize they are calling an internet phone?"*

He said, *"We do the quality testing ourselves. There are carrier options but it depends where you are located."*

Okay, still not helping me. One more try.

"Do you set up the carrier for your clients, or do you just recommend how they can do that?"

"We will do it for them. I use a VPN." He then rattled on for five minutes about things I didn't understand.

He knew nothing about me except my name at that point. And he clearly wasn't paying attention to whether his message was being understood.

I gave up and excused myself to get a drink.

Where did it fall apart for him?

He's in a business that many people won't understand, so he has two choices: he can ask me what I do so he can explain what he does relative to a business like mine; or he can explain it in a way that everyone can understand.

He went with option C ... talk at me until I couldn't take it anymore.

If you ever wonder why 'networking events don't work,' take a look at how you network.

When you speak, is it all about *you*?

Or do you carefully consider the person you're speaking with and what will matter to them?

If you haven't already figured out what problem you solve, that is your first step. The deeper you go to understand what you have to offer, the better you'll be able to influence people. In fact, the more you focus on finding your *ideal* people and presenting them with a *solution* to a problem they want to solve, the less selling you'll have to do. Your clients will just happen.

What's your big idea? How do you appeal to your clients?

Think about some of the great internationally known brands. What are their tag lines?

Apple, for example: *Think different*

They have also had: *Think outside the box* and *The power to be your best*.

These taglines are all about *their user*. In fact, they're about a core emotion of the user.

I converted to Apple about a year after I left my corporate job. There were practical reasons why I switched to a Mac – *stability* (programs like Garage Band and iMovie) and *speed*. But I also switched to Mac because I *identified* with the brand as someone who was ditching the norm and doing things differently.

That's who Apple is speaking to when they say 'Think different.' The products have become commonplace but the brand still speaks to artists, creators and entrepreneurs.

Here are a few others:

- Reach out and touch someone

- Eat fresh

- Because you're worth it

- I am Canadian.

AT&T really hits an emotional chord with their slogan. They solve the problem you have: that you are far away from your loved ones and you need to connect.

Subway knew that their customer wanted something that was perceived as healthy and yet still fast.

L'Oreal understands that they aren't selling make-up and creams. They are selling a feeling of beauty, of taking care of yourself, of being a desirable woman. They have found 'the big idea' as it relates to their customer.

Molson connected all Canadians with their 'I am Canadian' ads. We have an awesome country, and their ads had fun with stereotypes and hit our pride at a strong emotional level. It wasn't about their beer – it was about their *beer drinker.*

> *Having influence and an impact on others is all about knowing what is important to the person you want to persuade and putting it in a context that they can understand.*

So let's go back to my IT security and service guy. I don't truly understand what he does, so I have to take some liberties with this, but let's just try the whole conversation again from the point where he started to tell me what he did:

> Him: "Well it can be complicated, so it might help to know what business you are in, Julie."

> Me: "My main business is an education and training company. I help people who aren't comfortable selling create a strong personal brand so they have more influence, attract more clients, and boost their income. I am also a real estate investor – you know, collecting houses and renting them out."

> Him: "Oh – interesting. So in your education business, are you doing much online?"

> Me: "Yes. I travel all over North America to give talks, but most of the training I offer is delivered online through a membership portal."

> Him: "Wow! Storage must be a challenge for you then, with all those large video files? That's actually in line with what I do

in my business. I check the security and quality of my clients'
storage and internet services. I also do a lot around improving
the quality of VoIP. Do you know what that is?"

Can you see how we're having a conversation, and he has now set it up so he can put his business in a context that I will understand? And once I understand, there is a possibility he might uncover an area where he could help me.

It would have been a totally different conversation, and he may have walked out of that networking event with a new client.

UNDERSTAND THEIR PAIN

What is the core emotion that drives the customer to choose your product, or to work with you?

I am not looking for toothpaste. I want fresh breath and I want my teeth to look good when I smile.

But, it's more than that.

WHY do I want fresh breath and to look good when I smile?

If I'm an eye doctor, maybe it's so I don't knock my patients over with bad breath when I move in close to examine their eyes. Or maybe it's so I am attractive to my husband.

Or, maybe it's not for me at all. Maybe it's so I protect my kids' teeth from disease or damage that will be expensive and painful to fix.

When you're looking for a new job, do the same thing. Maybe the company is hiring a new office manager. Why do they *really* want an office manager? Sure, it might be to organize files and make sure they are never out of paper or coffee – but again, why?

Is it so the lawyers who make $200 an hour never have to spend a minute worrying about things like that? Once you understand *why* they really need someone in that position, you can start to get inside their minds to influence them as to why *you* are the right choice.

 Get into the deeper reasons why someone wants to have a product or a service. Then you can start to work on your big idea.

1. **How will my ideal client *identify* with what I am offering?**

   This goes back to understanding your ideal client. If you don't, as in the case of the IT Security example, then you need to spend some time to understand who you are speaking with, so you can find a way to help them identify with your offering. If you don't understand the person you're trying to connect with and that shows through in your marketing efforts, your material will fall flat and not attract any business.

   You may not always be speaking with your ideal person, but understanding what core emotional reason would make someone want to work with you or use your product is really important in determining if your brand is the solution to their problem.

2. **How will my ideal client remember me?**

   This goes back to how they will identify with what you offer, but giving them a one-liner that refers to the big idea of how you are helping them is what you want to do.

   As a full-time real estate investor, I often told people that I liked to "collect houses." People often remembered that because it was unique. I once met a woman who helps people handle relationship issues with their horses. She called herself a 'horse whisperer.' What can you say that is short and memorable about who you are and what you do?

3. **How will this benefit them?**

Again, the big idea is never about *you*. It's not about your business or you getting the job. The big idea is what *you* can do for *them*, and ideally it's something that other people can't do, at least not like you can. What will happen if they don't hire you or work with you? What are the risks? And, of course, what are the enormous benefits that you or your product can offer them?

IS SELLING BAD?

Once you know how you're helping others, and you know who your ideal client is, you still have to get comfortable *telling* people about it.

Scott Sylvan Bell, a great sales trainer (scottbellconsultant.com) shared this exercise. He said:

Take out a pen and paper.

Write down the first word that comes to your mind when you think of a sales person.

Go ahead. You can do this too. What's your word? Write it here:

The words that came up when I asked the group at one of my workshops were:

- Pushy

- Slimy

- Successful

- Not trustworthy

- Greedy

- Wealthy

- Confident

If your word was something like slimy, pushy or greedy, do you think that is having a negative impact on *your* ability to influence others?

Many people think of selling as something that is bad. But, it's really all about your *intention*.

If you are selling something that will benefit someone, and you do it with the person's best interest in mind, aren't you really just helping?

You should *want* to see people benefiting from what you offer. You should feel excited to share it with others.

Maybe your new words for a salesperson could be:

- Personable

- Great communicator

- Outgoing

- Helpful

- Patient

- Caring

- Results oriented

You have a gift to give others – but at first not everyone knows they need you. You have to help them see it.

In this book, we've covered a lot of ground already.

First, you've identified who you most want to work with and who you are best suited to help (your ideal client).

Second, you've opened your eyes so you're on the lookout for this ideal person. You are better equipped to see the person when they are in front of you, and to identify opportunities to help the person even more.

Third, you're going to put what you offer in the context that is most important to this person. Every conversation is about the person you're speaking with. It's *not* about you. And that's true even if the 'conversation' is via email or via your website.

With that done, it's time to get really clear on what elements you want to focus on for your brand, and then make your brand *known*. If you want people to come to you, ask to work with you, and tell others about you, there's some work you need to do upfront. This is where you can create a big advantage for yourself, because most people aren't willing to take the steps that make selling themselves easier and more comfortable.

That's what we're going to cover next.

 KEY ACTION ITEMS:

- Are you speaking in a context that your audience can relate to and understand, or is it all about *you*?

- Understand their pain. Identify the deeper reasons why someone needs your product or service. Specifically ask yourself:

  > How will my ideal client *identify* with what I am offering?

  > How will my client remember me?

  > How will this benefit them?

- What word do I associate with sales? What word do I want to associate with sales going forward?

CHAPTER 4

Aim Higher

When I was a young girl playing in the back yard of my parents' 20-room prairie town motel, I dreamed about being an astronomer, a teacher, and a writer. Sometimes I pictured the company that I would run. I didn't dream of working ten hours a day building someone else's company. Not once.

Yet, at the age of 30, I found myself doing just that.

I lost interest in astronomy when I found out how much math was involved. But somehow my childhood dreams of writing, teaching, and running my own business turned into dreams of earning a six-figure salary.

I wonder why I set the bar so low.

As Philip McKernan (PhilipMckernan.com) says, *"Most people are chasing goals that do not belong to them."*

Business school – of which I attended two, one for a BComm and one for an MBA – trains you to be a good employee. The entrepreneurial classes I audited were basically teaching you how to attract venture capital, not how to actually *run* a business that creates a life you want to live.

School teaches you to fit in; education comes with restrictions.

It's not bad. I love learning. I don't regret getting educated in post-secondary institutions, but I didn't really enjoy it. I could have created the life I have today without two degrees. But at some point I heard my family talking about how writers and teachers don't make money. As a teenager trying to figure out what I wanted to do with my life, I often overheard my parents and grandparents raving about how successful one of my cousins was. They proudly shared how great her job was and how much money she was making after having just completed her MBA.

My Mom always told me I could be anything I wanted to be. Those weren't just words. I know my parents would have supported almost *any* choice I made. But, as a young girl who wanted to make her family proud, it seemed a sure path to their praise was to follow in my cousin's footsteps ... so, for a while, I did.

 Where did your goals come from? Why are they important to you?

What else might be possible?

I love reading about Elon Musk, creator of Tesla and SpaceX, because he sets goals nobody thinks are possible and he goes for it. Few of us possess his level of genius or his ability to risk it all, but *what if we just dreamed a little bigger?*

What if we all set goals that *scared* us, even a little?

SETTING BORING GOALS

Are you familiar with the SMART goal-setting framework?

> Specific
> Measurable
> Achievable
> Relevant
> Time-based

When this framework was created in the 80's, it may have served an important purpose for managers of companies to set the goals for their teams, but take another look at that framework.

How do you *feel* when you read those words?

The words themselves are dry and boring. It's a very practical way to approach the task of goal setting, and it can be useful; but it's hardly going to get you leaping out of bed onto a cold floor in the middle of winter, is it?

I'm not going to try to recreate the SMART framework, but play along with me just for a second. Let's pretend that framework was actually to set goals that met these criteria:

> Scary, exciting
> Motivating
> Action oriented
> Really easy to visualize
> Tied to a greater vision.

Now, how do you feel when you read those words? You feel them in your gut, don't you? There's possibility, opportunity and desire buried in those words.

Mark Murphy, author of *HARD Goals*, uses a simple question to test whether someone will achieve their goal, or not. He asks them:

> *Why do you care about this goal?*

That's an *emotional* question to test the *power* of someone's goal – because we're *emotional*. We're not *rational* like the original SMART framework suggests.

If we were rational, we'd never eat potato chips or donuts, or drink vodka. We'd exercise daily, consume a lot more vegetables, and drink a lot more water.

Murphy also talks about the *necessity* of a difficult goal – something scary and important. He says: *"When you set a difficult goal, it consumes so much of your brain's resources that it crowds out a lot of other less important stuff. It's like shutting down some of those background computer applications. And with that extra brainpower comes better performance."*[6]

Sure, a goal that is specific and measurable is easy to tick off a list, but it's boring. Goals that are easily achievable won't hit the mark; your brain is not forced to perform at an optimal level to get there. And a deadline means nothing if you can't see what success looks like and how it fits in to creating the life you really want to live.

In his book *From Good to Great*, Jim Collins introduced the idea of "BHAG" for corporate goals. BHAG stands for <u>B</u>ig <u>H</u>airy <u>A</u>udacious <u>G</u>oal. Your BHAG is at the intersection of what you care about passionately, what you can be the best in the world at, and what drives your economic engine.

Elon Musk sets Big Hairy Audacious Goals. He revolutionizes any industry he touches. His latest obsession is making man a multi-planetary species. He has the attitude, money and extraordinary intelligence to make it happen. And the financial potential of what he's doing is enormous. Take the latest development toward reusable rockets with the successful landing of the Falcon 9. A rocket that costs 16 million dollars to manufacture can now be reused because it wasn't lost or destroyed in space like other rockets. That means a dramatic reduction in cost and will quickly change the face of the private space industry.[7]

That's the kind of goal that is scary, motivating, easy to visualize, and tied to a greater vision.

You don't have to change the world, or the face of space travel, but if you want a brand that is memorable and meaningful, you do need to

---

6 Mark Murphy, *Hard Goals*, (Toronto: McGraw Hill, 2011), 142.

7 http://www.theverge.com/2015/12/21/10640306/spacex-elon-musk-rocket-landing-success

set a goal that gets you fired up. Can you see how it's going to positively impact others, create a life you want, and make life more interesting? If you're answering YES, then you're much more likely to leap out of bed to get to it every single day.

TO WIN, YOU NEED CHIPS IN THE CENTER

I've been learning to play No Limit Texas Hold'em Poker. Nick Binger, the instructor at the World Poker Tour Cash Camp I took, said *"Make the right decisions and you can expect to win about 60% of the time."* He laughed and then asked, "So how often does it feel like you're losing if you're winning 60% of the time?"

Losing 40% of the time will feel like losing 90% of the time.

Yet, winning 60% of the time means you're making progress.

The thought of failing 40% of the time is scarier than winning 60% of the time.

We're taught to play it safe.

> *This kind of programming makes setting great goals more difficult. We want to protect ourselves from loss more than we want to push for the big payday.*

Poker teaches you that the *only* way you can get the big payday is to be okay with the losses along the way. You'll never win in Poker if your chips aren't in the middle. The goal is to minimize your losses and maximize your wins.

With poker there is a visible cost to doing nothing. In life, when you delay important decisions, you pay, but it's not always easy to *see* the cost.

Poker shows you how expensive it is to do nothing. Every 15 minutes or so, when you're playing a cash game, you will have to put in the blinds (essentially a forced bet). If you play the lowest stakes (called a 1-2 game), every hour you sit at the table and do nothing costs you $9-$12.

Because their chip stack is dwindling, most players take action even when conditions aren't perfect, trying to create opportunities. They won't sit on the sidelines doing nothing because it's expensive.

If only we all had this *real cost* right in front of us every day, we might not be so reserved in what we do with our lives.

Not every moment is a good one to make a bet, but you must decide when the time *is* right and then just go for it. Make a big bet on yourself; your situation will never be perfect, so jump in.

GOING ALL IN

The day I sat down with my boss and gave my notice was the day I went 'all in' for myself.

The market conditions and my own financial situation were far from ideal for me to leave. It was 2008. The market was horrible for what *I* wanted to do – build two businesses in real estate. But, there were three things that made me leave without hesitation.

First, I couldn't stay where I was any longer. I realized the only way to create the life I wanted was to leave and figure it out from there.

Second, I had the full support of my husband to leave, even though we were living on my salary at the time. The fact that he never doubted me when I told him I was going to quit gave me so much belief in myself.

Third, we owned a dozen investment properties at the time. The massive downturn in real estate prices was just starting to hit Canada, but knowing we had some equity to fall back on gave us some comfort. We could sell a property or two (and we did) to survive while we built up our income.

It was not easy. My first book, *More than Cashflow*, covers all the challenges we faced as we became full time real estate investors. We turned our home, complete with all our kitchen stuff, furniture and appliances, into a furnished rental and moved back in with my parents for two years to make it work. Strangers slept in our bed and ruined our couch, but the gift I gave myself was one that nobody can ever take away – an unwavering belief that I can do what I set my mind to do.

At some point you have to make a leap. You will have to either go all in, or lose time and money as you watch the opportunities pass you by.

Seth Godin wrote a cool little book called *Poke the Box*. He states that in order to create anything remarkable in your life and business, you must *initiate*. You have to be willing to fail and to be blamed.

Initiative is scarce and that makes it enormously valuable.[8]

Find the thing that gets you jazzed up, scares you, and helps you create a life that you're excited to live.

It's amazing what shows up in your life when you do this.

ARE YOU READY TO DO WHATEVER IT TAKES?

George Bernard Shaw has been quoted as saying *"Doing what needs to be done may not make you happy but it will make you great."*

I heard Gary Vaynerchuk speak at the *Thrive* event in Las Vegas. He said:

> *A lot of people want to know the secret to getting a million Twitter followers.*

---

8   Seth Godin, *Poke the Box*, (USA: Do You Zoom Inc., 2011)

Here it is: I spent 15 hours a day on Twitter replying to every single person who tweeted about wine. I was on Twitter so much my eyes were bleeding.

Few people do what it takes. That's why so many personal brands are so blah!

A lot of people try to *fit in*, and then wonder why they don't *stand out*!

In 2014, I ran a course to help real estate investors create a *brand* to make it easier to raise money for their deals. As part of the class, every person had the opportunity to write an article for my newsletter and website, *revnyou.com*. The newsletter had close to 10,000 active readers at the time. I told the class that one of my guest writers who had written an article earlier that year attracted an investor to finance a $300,000 property because of the article.

There were 14 people in the class. How many people submitted a proposal? I would have guessed that about half the class would take me up on the offer.

I would have been wrong.

Gillian Irving was the only one in the group of fourteen people who submitted a proposal and then wrote an article.

Since then, she's been on some big stages across Canada as a featured expert on Student Rentals. She's been featured in *Canadian Real Estate Wealth Magazine* and has partnered with a few other smart and savvy women to teach and coach other women investors. She and these women are now regulars on media outlets in Toronto talking about investing.

I'm not saying that these things happened because of the article. I'm saying that these things happened to her because she steps up and does the work.

Very few people are willing to stretch even a little to create success.

They have really rational sounding 'reasons' why they don't do the work, but those are *excuses*. Period.

We are all ordinary people, but it's possible to do extraordinary things.

You have a choice. *The first step is believing that YOU can live another way and that you're worth an 'all-in bet.'*

After that, it's a little trickier, but asking some good questions will help.

When I quit my job, I had to generate income fast. My husband and I did that in two ways:

1. Raising a significant amount of money in order to grow our real estate portfolio – specifically with rent-to-own deals and houses with suites.

2. Turning our free real estate investing newsletter into a training and education company.

Figuring out *how* to do that was a little more difficult. Thankfully my parents signed me up for some business mentoring with Keith J. Cunningham. He provided a lot of sound advice and asked some great questions. In particular, there were seven questions that have helped me a lot since I learned them in 2009.

 Before you move on to the next chapter, sit down with pen and paper and write the answers to these seven questions (worksheets available at TheNewBrandYou.com).

1. **Where would I like to be one year from today? What do I want most of my working days to look like, and what does an ideal day look like?**

    Again – this question isn't asking you what you will make money doing. Of course, you have to figure that part out, but *what do you really want to do*?

2. Why am I not there now? (List all the reasons)

This is a great question to remind you that the thinking that got you to where you are today is *not* what is going to get you where you want to go. What have you not yet done?

3. What am I assuming to be true? And if it wasn't true, would it change my approach and my thinking?

Maybe you assume that you need a business degree. Or that you need to be technically skilled, or that you could do it if you were from a different family. Dig deep and be honest: what are you assuming to be true?

We all make assumptions. My biggest one back in 2008 was that I didn't have enough real estate investing experience to teach others, or even to raise the kind of money we wanted to raise. This question helped me to put in perspective the education and experience that we *did* have and who we were very well equipped to help.

Imagine if Arnold Schwarzenegger had made assumptions in his life! He had to face non-stop limitations, starting with his life in Austria where he had to go AWOL from the army to attend his first bodybuilding competition.[9]

And he could have let any number of assumptions hold him back from moving to the US, including the fact that he hardly spoke any English. But if he had never moved to the US, he never would have trained under Joe Wieder in Venice, California, and he would

---

9   http://www.latimes.com/entertainment/tv/showtracker/la-et-donald-vs-arnold-comparing-the-once-and-future-celebrity-apprentice-hosts-20150914-htmlstory.html

likely not have been Mr. Olympia seven times over. Nor would he have become one of the most famous movie stars of the 90's, married into one of America's most famous families, or become Governor of the largest state in the US. Every dream he had presented massive challenges, but clearly he's a man who doesn't let obstacles hold him back.

4. What tradeoffs and sacrifices are required to make progress toward achieving my goal?

So you want to play it safe? Or you don't want to spend money on training or a mentor? Or you're too nervous to pursue an idea you have for fear it won't work? Fine – get comfortable and content with the way you live today.

Everything you want has a price. If you're not willing to pay the price, you won't get what you want.

This question doesn't ask what you are *willing* to do; it asks what tradeoffs are *required*. You can't get fit by eating a lot of donuts.

To start a business, you have to put in time, energy and resources. If you have a full-time job and a family, you're going to have to sacrifice some sleep, a few family dinners, recreation time, friend time, and probably some income because you may have to reduce your hours so you can focus on your side business. That's what is *required* if you want to succeed.

5. What activity or skill must I excel at to achieve my goal?

There are always a lot of things that you need to do, but there is typically one single skill that is holding you back from your true potential.

For many, it's the ability to communicate what you do and how you can help.

If you can *sell* yourself, your service or your product, you will succeed.

When it comes to creating a great personal brand, you can hire out almost every aspect of it, *except* when you need to be face-to-face speaking with someone. In that case, your success will depend on your ability to communicate what you do in a compelling way.

6. **What are the things I will measure to gauge my progress?**

   Keith Cunningham calls them *critical drivers*. These are the things that *drive* both sales and expenses.

   The number of new leads that come in each day and the percentage that converts to clients would be a driver of sales. Another driver might be the number of hours spent on marketing specific activities. The more time spent writing high value content, creating promotions, giving talks, and speaking on podcasts and webinars, the more leads that will come into the business. The number of leads will have a direct result on how much money you will be able to generate in the next three months.

   One driver of expenses might be the cost per unit of materials used to create your product. If that goes up, the expenses go up across the board.

   The key for a business is to measure which activities have the biggest impact. You have to figure out what drives your business and what you'll measure each month in order to know if your business is heading in the right direction.

For example, do you know where your *best* leads come from? If you aren't tracking which leads become clients, then you might know which source sends you the largest number of leads, but you won't know what your *best* source is. If you've been tracking, you may find out that your best source of leads comes from the cold calls you make to event organizers looking to book your DJ services. If that is the case, you need to measure how many calls you make each month.

If you're a nutritionist, and your best source of business is the tradeshows you attend, you'll want to measure how many tradeshows you participate in every month. These may also be your greatest driver of expenses, so you'll be tracking how much you spend per tradeshow to identify the ones with the best return.

7. **If your friend asked you for advice regarding the same goal that *you're* trying to achieve, what advice would you give them?**

We all have fears, and it's natural to avoid our fears, so if you look at your situation as though it were your friend's, you may see something you were avoiding. When you realize what advice you'd give to a friend, you're more likely to face the issue that's holding *you* back.

My heart still races at the poker table when I go 'all-in,' just like it races when I commit to something that scares me in my life and in business. Sometimes it doesn't work out, but I'm almost always glad I took the risk.

The question isn't whether you can or can't have what you want. The question is *what are you willing to do to get it*? What will it cost in terms of time, energy and money to get what you want? Are you willing to push all your chips into the center and go all-in on yourself?

The big difference between your life and poker is that in poker your chips are probably a non-renewable resource. In life, *your energy is renewable.* Push yourself hard – do whatever it takes. If you don't get there today, have a good dinner and a great sleep, and pick up where you left off tomorrow.

Grant Cardone, in his hard-hitting book, *The 10x Rule,* says that your success depends on your ability to increase your *efforts* – not your excuses. Don't adjust your target – adjust your action!

If you really want something in your life, commit to doing whatever it takes. A great life is available to you – go get it!

Not sure what exactly to do? Keep reading ... we're getting into it.

 KEY ACTION ITEM:

- Ditch your boring goals and set a Big Goal that is going to scare you, get you excited, and have a positive impact, and that is easy to visualize.

- **You're worth an all-in bet – what do you want your life to look like?**

CHAPTER 5

You Are Who Google Says You Are

"The strangest part about being famous is that you don't get to give first impressions anymore. Everyone already has an impression of you before you meet them."

Kristen Stewart

When was the last time you Googled your own name?

Go ahead ... try it right now.

What shows up on the first page?

What are the first couple of links? Are they you?

More importantly than you actually showing up, is that you are pleased with what is there. Does it reflect the brand image you're aiming for?

Your first impression is the one you make (or don't make) online.

Just about everyone is entering your name into Google to learn about you before they meet you. Many are finding you (or, not finding you) when they want to do business with someone in your industry. Your online impression is becoming more and more important every day.

In early 2016, Apple quietly announced the purchase of a company that uses artificial intelligence to read faces and decode body language. Facebook and Google have already reported working on their own similar software.[10]

You can already do reverse image look-ups online, so it won't be long before every smart phone or Google Glass product can search for your online profile as you walk into a room!

The day might not be here yet, but it's close. Your personal brand is already being impacted by what is (and, is not) found online. It's only going to become more important. It's time to pay close attention and start tweaking it to reflect exactly who you are in order to attract the business and clients you want.

DO YOU PASS THE GOOGLE TEST TODAY?

"Hmm, what was her name?" I thought as I opened up Google.

"I think it was Jane Olsen,[11] but is it Olsen with an e, or Olson with an o...?"

I entered the first option into the search bar.

A Facebook link was first, so I clicked that.

> *"She's in the right city, but this can't possibly be the real estate professional my friend told me about. There's nothing 'real estate' here ... just cats, tattoos and concerts."*

I click back to the Google search results.

The next link goes to the results of a running race. The next link is for a city petition. There are eight results, but none seem to fit.

---

10 http://www.wired.com/2016/01/apple-buys-ai-startup-that-reads-emotions-in-faces/

11 Not her real name.

This isn't working, so I try the other version of the name with 'realtor' beside it.

Ten minutes later, I haven't found Jane, but I did find another real estate agent who had some interesting blog posts, so I reached out to him instead.

Jane failed the Google test. Make sure you don't miss out on business because of your Google test results.

Your ideal client will probably look for you online. Make sure you can be found.

Now let's find any potential issues you may have....

1. **Is your name easy for people to remember so they know what to search?**

   It's been almost ten years since I lived in or purchased real estate in Toronto. Despite the big gap in activity, I still remember Margie K.

   The funny part is that Margie K wasn't even my realtor. She was my friend's realtor.

   Her last name is long and very difficult to spell so she decided to go with Margie K.

   Smart move. It worked.

   If you Google 'Margie K Realtor' the entire page is full of links that lead you to her.

   My friend, business coach and consultant Deborah Cole, goes by Coach Deb. When she's networking, that is how she introduces herself. That's her Twitter handle. Her website is coachdeb.tv. Her name is simple, personable and concise. 'Coach Deb' is easy to remember and smart branding.

   In an ideal world, people will text or email your contact information to others, but it often doesn't happen that way! So, if you're name is not easy or memorable, come up with another way for people to remember you and refer to you.

2. **What will people find when they Google you?**

Google will show results for images as well. Make sure you're paying attention to *all* the results that show up under your name.

What if that first Jane Olsen actually was the realtor I was looking for? I don't think it was, but with party pictures, tattoos and cats being the focus of what I found, I certainly wouldn't think she was the expert real estate professional I was looking for.

If you aren't showing up in the first three links when someone searches your name, then you need to do a better job of controlling your online presence. And if something you're not happy about is showing up, do everything in your power to change or remove it (for example, remove tags on Facebook photos, delete the source of the content, or bury that link).

How?

The first step is to own yourname.com (yourname.ca if you live in Canada) and your personalized links on Facebook, LinkedIn and Twitter.

You don't have to be overly active on social media to take advantage of the opportunity social media offers to control more Google Search results. You just need a well-thought-out profile with your name and some contact information so your searchers can get to your website or to your email and phone number.

Google owns YouTube and, of course, Google+, and these links often show up on page 1. If you're trying to bury links, a few Google+ posts with your name, or a popular YouTube video, could bump the unwanted links down a few spots.

What does 'bury a link' mean?

Let's say there's a media story that misquotes what you said. Or, there's a bad customer review on a blog that doesn't tell the whole story. Or, your high school yearbook picture comes up, and you just don't want your love of piercings when you were 18 to be the first thing potential clients or business partners see.

If these things aren't on sites that you can control, you can contact the site owner and ask them to remove it; however, you might not have much luck. In that case, your only option is to bury them deep in the Google Search results so people would have to go several pages deep to find them. That's where social media profiles, your own website, YouTube videos and other media content will really help you online.

What if someone else owns your name as a URL right now (for example, JulieBroad.com)?

i.   Check the URL to see if it's in use.

ii. If there is a website but it hasn't been updated for years, try to contact the owner of the website. If there isn't contact information on their site or there isn't a live website at the URL, you can try looking them up through sites like whois.net or betterwhois.com. If the registration is private, you can use a broker or go through a site like namecheap.com to try to have the owner contacted so you can ask to buy the domain. One of my coaching clients did that and was able to buy his name for $100. That's money well spent to control your brand.

iii. If someone else is actively using your name – especially if it's used with .com or .ca – get creative with your branding and that URL, for example, Margie K or Coach Deb. My friend (and a smart sales trainer and speaker) Scott Bell has this challenge and he uses his middle name, Scott Sylvan Bell instead. With that locked down, *consistency* is now the key. It won't work if you're 'MargieK.com' but then everywhere else you use your full name. *All* of your marketing, networking and other online sites need to reflect the name you've chosen. Of course you will be required to use your full name for some sites, like LinkedIn, for example, but your branding and images on that page must reflect the brand name you've chosen.

iv. The research you did in Step 2 will tell you when the URL registration expires. Put that date in your calendar and check back. JulieBroad.com was owned and used by a psychologist in Australia for a period of time, but I kept checking back and after a few years I was able to grab and purchase my name.

3. Is it easy for people to *connect* with you?

This is meant in two ways: can they physically find your contact information *and* do they emotionally connect with you and your message?

Ask your friends and colleagues what they think when they Google your name. Is it easy to find your contact information? Do they quickly get a sense of who you are and the kind of service you offer?

One of my personal pet peeves is not being able to quickly find a picture of someone when I visit their website. Even if it's a company, I want to see who works there. Considering that the 'About' page on both of my websites is the second most visited page, I know that I am not the only one looking to answer 'Who is this person?'

Think about your *ideal client*. What are they going to want to see when they search your name? What problems will they be actively trying to solve online?

Is it clear how you can help them solve that problem?

Can they easily connect with you to do that?

SHOULD I WAIT UNTIL I AM READY?

You might think that your idea, your product, your service, or whatever you offer isn't big enough, or that you're not experienced enough, so therefore you should wait to create your online profile, build a website, or put yourself out as your new brand; *but if you know you can help others, what are you waiting for?*

Sloppy success is better than perfect mediocrity[12]

Seth Godin talks about the importance of 'shipping' in his book *Linchpin*. He says there's a shortage of people who create solutions and hustle them out the door. Sometimes *shipping* feels like a compromise because it's not perfect, but Godin suggests it's more important to have the habit of *shipping* than it is to have everything right.

In her book *Big Magic*, Elizabeth Gilbert shares that there's a character in her New York bestselling novel *The Signature of All Things* that was left underdeveloped. She acknowledges "her presence is little more than a convenience to the plot."[13] She knew that this character wasn't quite right, but she thought she'd try to sneak it by the readers. The early reader feedback noted the character underdevelopment, and she considered revising the story before publishing, but she said it would have required dismantling a big portion of the book. She decided to leave it. In her mind, it was 'good enough.'

> *"It was time for me to shift my attention to something new – something that would also, someday, be released as 'good enough.' That is how I've always done it, and this is how I will keep doing it, as long as I am able."*[14]

Apple clearly agrees with this philosophy as well. Nothing is perfect when they ship it, but if they waited until it was perfect, their competition would crush them. I've downloaded so many of their operating systems that had dozens of glitches. Bit by bit they would sort them out and fix them – but they didn't wait to deliver; they shipped and then perfected.

---

12 We heard Alex Mandossian, online marketer, use this expression at an Early to Rise event in 2007. It may not have been his quote originally, but we always think of him as the one who said it.

13 Elizabeth Gilbert, *Big Magic* (New York: Riverhead Books, 2015), 178

14 Gilbert, p. 181

Live news shows have to go on every day – perfect or not.

So, your message, service or product might not be perfect. There will always be some things about your website you want to change, so just hit 'publish,' and stop wasting time trying to create the perfect business card. (If you're easy to find and connect with online, you don't even need a business card anymore!)

Who needs your help *right* now? Focus on helping that person.

Then move forward from there. Even when you create entertainment products like movies, books or radio shows, it's not about *you*. It's not *for* you.

The focus of this book is on reaching and connecting with others to have more impact and influence. It's about having conversations and communicating what you have to offer – in an interesting and clear way.

Although the primary focus of this book is not *making money*, it's interesting *how much money people can make* when they are open about who they are and clear on how they serve others.

So think about who needs to hear what you have to say. **Who could be living a better life if they just learned what you have to teach, heard your story, or used the product you have to offer?**

DO YOU HAVE THE RIGHT MARKETING STRATEGY?

Have you heard something like this lately?

> *What you **do** need, however, is the right strategy.*
> *Strategy. Is. Everything.*

Those words are from an email that hit my inbox with the goal of selling a video marketing course.

As I read the email, I realized I have been hearing this word 'strategy' a lot lately.

Last week, an applicant for a licensee program to teach our real estate courses asked, *"What should my main strategy be to get a good ROI on this?"*

I sent him an email and asked, *"Do you like teaching and helping people?"*

His reply was quick: *"Not like you do! You seem to live for it. I want to use the right strategy so I don't have to spend a lot of time doing this."*

I politely ended the exchange, suggesting that he pursue something that he was more interested in.

What do you *like* to do?

What did you *love* to do when you were a kid, before you worried about your responsibilities or about being a grown up?

When I was a little kid, my parents hung a giant green chalkboard in our patio room for me to use. After school, I would either be at my desk writing a story, or I would sit my younger brother down in front of that chalkboard and teach him the cool things I'd learned at school that day. If he wasn't into listening, I would line up my stuffed animals and teach *them*.

People often think I am more strategic in business than I actually am.

I am organized in my thinking. When I commit to doing something – I do it. I am disciplined by nature. I care immensely about other people – especially people who place their trust in me. It's almost a weakness that I care so much. More than once, I've reached a point of burnout by giving too much of my time to others and focusing on all the things I can do to help them get where they want to go.

This isn't a business strategy though – this is who I am.

I usually consider someone's situation and try to identify how I can personally help them move forward. I think about a client's problems when I go for a run. I ponder the potential of people I work with. I introduce my clients to people who can help them – with no expectation of getting anything in return (although I do really appreciate it when someone thanks me). I send them ideas and help them open doors. If I can do something for a friend or client that will help in a big way, I will. I do it because I care.

If you're getting into coaching and training because the money is good, you won't succeed. Most people will sense that you are in it for the money.

Even if you do make a great ROI, you're going to be doing something you don't enjoy. Is that really success?

I have a friend and client who loves to write. He used to write a newsletter purely for the enjoyment of it. He stopped because he didn't know if anybody was reading it or getting any value from it. When I suggested he return to writing the newsletter, he wondered what the *strategy* would be for doing it.

I get where he's coming from. The message that you need to be strategic is everywhere. I've even used it in my own marketing without thinking about it! But I think the pursuit of the right *strategy* is failing a lot of people.

Strategy. Is. Not. Everything.

If you don't like to do something – the right strategy won't change that.

For every 'sure-fire marketing strategy' you learn, you'll find people succeeding who do it in an opposite way. You'll also find people implementing the strategy perfectly and not succeeding.

There are marketing reasons for writing a regular newsletter, but that isn't the first reason to do it.

We launched our first newsletter in April of 2006. We didn't make a single penny from that newsletter until 2009. And, frankly, even if we hadn't turned it into a business, I'd still be writing a newsletter.

I wanted to do it. I wanted to share, and I hoped it helped people.

So if you hate social media but you Tweet, Pin, Blab, Snap and post to Facebook because it's part of a sound business strategy, stop! See if someone else in your business likes doing it and will do it on behalf of your business, or just stop worrying about it. Yes, it can be great for a business, but not if the person doing it sees it as a chore! There are far more important things you can be doing.

Maybe you like meeting new people, hosting parties or playing sports. Have you ever thought of how you could bring those things into your marketing? Maybe you love painting or singing – have you considered how this could be brought into what you do?

If you don't want to do it – find another way to get where you want to go.

Marketing is not about boring print ads or interrupting someone's favorite radio or TV show with a commercial.

Marketing – especially when it comes to your brand – is all about connection, engagement, and entertainment!

You probably have some cool talents, interests and/or personality traits that could be great marketing assets if people were given the chance to see them.

You don't need a new strategy. You need a new approach *that fits with who you are and what you like to do.*

There are things in business that have to be done – like sitting 'on hold' with tech support when your computer stops working, paying bills, reviewing financial statements, paying taxes, and setting up systems so things work properly. I suffer through these things because ultimately they allow me to do more of the things I love to do – write, speak and teach to impact others.

I'm not suggesting that if you simply be yourself, you'll make a lot more money. You might, but you still have to deliver *value*. There will still be work to do!

What I'm suggesting is that you're probably thinking about having the 'right' strategy way more than you need to. What you need to do is connect more to the things you *like* to do and disconnect more from the things you really don't like to do.

So, what do you *love* to do? Can you bring that into your business? What your business needs is a lot more of THE REAL YOU – *online and offline*.

 KEY ACTION ITEMS:

- Google Your Name – What comes up?

- After chatting with someone you've just met for a few minutes, ask them to do you a favor and pull out their phone and Google you. When they go to do it, can they remember your name? Or do they have trouble spelling it?

- If you aren't happy with what shows up on Google, what are three things you're going to do *this week* to improve the results? What are three things you're going to do *this month* to improve the results?

- What is something you love to do that you could bring into your business to increase the connection you have with others?

CHAPTER 6

The Brand Magic Formula

"Research has demonstrated that a shocking percentage of viewers remember your commercial, but forget the name of your product. All too often they attribute your commercial to a competing brand."

David Ogilvy in *Ogilvy on Advertising*

IS YOUR NAME HELPING OR HURTING YOUR BRAND?

How many times do you forget someone's name right after they've said it? You might remember the context of how you met them. You might even remember the color of the shirt they were wearing, but their name isn't there.

A person's name is one of the most powerfully persuasive words you can use, so finding a way to remember names is a good habit to get into. For now, let's focus on the fact that the people you're meeting will forget *your* name if you haven't considered how you're going to be remembered.

If you have a difficult name, come up with a way for people to remember you. You could suggest something it rhymes with or a funny cliché that people can associate with your name. After 30 years with the same last name, I was pretty attached to it, but that was not the only reason I kept it when I got married. I get a lot of mileage out of being 'a Broad.' I can make a lot of jokes about being 'a Broad' and about having 'Broad Shoulders.' If I can make someone smile, it can make me more memorable. Peniuk, my husband's last name, is a fine last name, but for me, it lacks the brand appeal that Broad has.

The name you choose to go by is powerful. You can have a pen name or a stage name, or just tweak how you refer to yourself in your marketing to make yourself easier to remember. Many famous people have done it over the years....

Do you know who Anthony J. Mahavoric is? I'm sure you do; it's just that you don't know Tony Robbins by his birth name.

Do you know who *Stefani* Joanne Angelina Germanotta is? Lady Gaga even released one album under her real name, but you probably don't know about it because it wasn't a hit like her Lady Gaga material.

What about Katheryn Elizabeth Hudson? It's not the actress Kate Hudson. In fact, some sources say it's because of Kate Hudson that she doesn't go by that name; she knew it would be confusing. So when you hear any of Katy Perry's hits you now know what name she was born with.

And what about Eric Marlon Bishop? When Jamie Foxx started doing standup comedy, the female comedians were routinely called up first. He didn't like waiting that long, so instead of signing up as Eric he picked a more gender-neutral stage name so he would get called up sooner.[15]

Your name can be the reason why you do or don't get jobs, contracts or opportunities. If you've ever read anything by James Chartrand

---

15 https://www.yahoo.com/movies/bp/why-jamie-foxx-changed-
    name-200200773.html?nf=1

– from a brilliant blog called *Men with Pens* – you may be shocked to know that James is not a man; she's a woman.

Frustrated because nobody was accepting her pitches, she changed her name to James Chartrand, and suddenly proposals that had previously been rejected got accepted.

Beyond your name, what's the brand you want? What makes you special?

What feelings do people associate with you? What makes them think of you?

At a business mastermind meeting, each person in the group was asked to say one word they thought of when they looked at me. The words were almost all in alignment with my brand. The words were:

- Expert

- Effective

- Confident

- Calm

- Elegant

- Sincere

- Genuine

- Supportive

- Successful

The only word that I don't see as part of my brand is 'elegant.' Maybe that's because I have blisters on my hands from Crossfit, I'm incredibly clumsy, and I am always more casual than formal, but the word definitely isn't a bad one.

So, what are the eight to ten words you would want associated with YOUR brand?

That's not a rhetorical question....

 ## TIP

- Stop here. Get out your pen and paper and write the words.

- If you want to test the gap between the words you chose and what others would choose, you could reach out to clients and friends and acquaintances and ask them to share *one word* that comes to mind when they think of you.

- A personal brand isn't a logo. It's values. It's emotions. It's expertise. It's *you*.

YOU ARE YOUR BRAND

You can take the time and make an effort to develop a meaningful and memorable brand, *or* you can take the chance that you are naturally having a good impact.

However, few people will have a strong impact without an effort.

The celebrities with strong brands have worked hard to create their brand: Oprah, Taylor Swift, Katy Perry, the Kardashians, Donald Trump and Adam Levine all have strong brands, but not by accident.

Van Halen worked hard to create their image as self-absorbed and emotional rock stars. It may seem silly, but that reputation sold records!

Van Halen's contract had a rider specifying that *there were to be no brown M&Ms in their candy bowl*. No reason was given as to why this was important to them, but David Lee Roth was known to trash the dressing rooms if a single brown candy was found.

Fans loved it, and this became part of the legend of Van Halen. Decades later, Roth confessed that there wasn't a distaste for, or an allergy to, brown coloring. The band had really heavy equipment; and if the stage wasn't set up properly, the safety of fans and the band was at risk. The equipment details were outlined in their rider, along with the brown M&M request. Rather than check all the technical aspects of the equipment and stage set-up to ensure all their specifications were met, they would head straight to the candy bowl to see if the brown M&M's had been removed. If they had, they could relax, knowing that the concert promoter was paying attention to details and not trying to cut costs. If they found brown M&M's, they would often find that other details were missed and the concert promoter would pay for it.

When asked why he didn't set the record straight sooner, he confessed to the PR value, saying, *"Who am I to deny a good rumor?"*[16]

Creating your brand will take work. You're probably not going to trash dressing rooms to get attention, but you will have to try things out. You probably won't have it perfectly figured out when you first start putting your message out there; but as you listen to what people say and what they remember, you'll figure out what is connecting and what isn't. It's a process.

WHO YOU *BE* COMES FIRST

Running a business requires different skills than what I learned in business school. I learned how to spend million-dollar ad budgets, how to analyze large real estate developments, and how to write detailed consultant reports. I didn't learn how to generate $10,000 in sales with zero dollars to spend on marketing.

Transitioning from corporate business to entrepreneurial business required a few mindset shifts.

---

16 Steve Jones, *Start You Up: Rock Star Secrets to Unleash Your Personal Brand and Set Your Career on Fire.* (Austin, Texas: Greenleaf Book Press, 2014), 50.

One of the key mindset shifts was something that originated from Zig Ziglar, I believe; but I learned it from Keith Cunningham. It was:

'BE, DO, HAVE'

It's the reverse to how most of us approach life. Most of us approach our goals with the idea that *if we have x, we will do y and be z*. For example, I thought: when I **have** an MBA, I can **do** a job where I make six figures, and then I will **be** successful, have freedom and feel financially secure.

It doesn't work that way. In fact, that line of thinking often takes you in the entirely *wrong* direction. In my case, I woke up one day with a career I had never actually wanted.

The solution?

Figure out *who you want to 'be'* first.

The way Keith explained it to me was: *"who you **be** dictates what you **do**, and what you do dictates what you'll **have**."*

I think that's close. I actually think it's about connecting to who you actually **are** and letting yourself **be** that person. That will dictate what you **do**, and what you **have**.

Most of us resist who we really are.

We worry if we will be liked. For some of us, high school taught us to hide our opinions, dress like the most popular individuals, and, for goodness sake, *don't* appear like you're trying too hard.

With a lesson that hits so hard so early in life, no wonder we tend to hide our true selves. But it's too bad, and it holds us back.

Fear keeps you from stepping up and standing out. Society has a way of keeping most people 'in line.'

This causes everything in our lives to get really messed up.

I was never meant to work for someone else in a corporate job. I'm very independent. I like adventure, challenge, freedom and room to create.

Even having been raised by entrepreneurial parents, I still ended up following society's accepted path of going to school and getting a good job. My husband did too.

If I had figured out *who* I wanted to *be*, I never would have pursued an MBA. I would have found a way to turn my love for writing and teaching into a business much sooner than I did.

Consider carefully *who you are*. That's where you begin when you build your brand.

THE KEY ELEMENTS OF YOUR PERSONAL BRAND

So before we get into the common branding mistakes, what are the elements of your own personal brand that you should be considering? To help you get clear as you create your personal brand, I've developed the **Brand Magic Formula**:

1. MESSAGE – What You Say and How You Say It

To have a strong brand you need a clear, concise and consistent message. You also must choose which media are best for you to use to communicate, and what you can say and do to gain attention and connect with your ideal person. We're going to cover this in much greater detail in upcoming chapters. For now, let's focus on what you do when you first meet someone and how you're communicating your message.

We all want to do business with people we like, and you'll find that people like you more when they feel as if they know you, at least to some extent. Your goal isn't to share everything about yourself, however. Consider what will be of the most interest, or the most memorable to your audience; and generally focus on sharing those details.

You want to connect with your ideal person – and chances are your ideal person will have some things in common with you, so those personal details will help to create a better relationship. We're not even halfway through the book yet, and you already know about my love of Crossfit/fitness, Poker, books, and my family – which includes my two dogs. Those are the main things I share with people on a regular basis.

I've found that these interests are also easy to translate into lessons or stories that people can relate to – whether you know what Crossfit is or not.

So that's a bit about what you're talking about. How will people hear your message? How will people find out about you?

One way people will hear about you is through referrals. **Have you ever thought about the story that is getting told when you are referred to someone?** Rarely will someone just give your name when they refer you. They will tell a short story about why their friend or colleague should connect with you or trust you to help them.

Put yourself in the driver's seat regarding what stories get told by giving your audience the stories they can then share with others (we have an entire section coming up on the stories you will tell).

Are you delivering your message from a stage, or on a website, or with social media, videos, articles, or smoke signals?

How your message gets delivered is a pretty important consideration. Marie Forleo is known for her videos. John Lee Dumas is known for his podcasts. Tim Ferris is a writer at the heart of all that he does. What will you enjoy doing, and where are you best able to connect with your ideal prospects?

I'm a big fan of video and speaking, and I enjoy most aspects of creating content for talks and videos, but I'm a writer first. If you hate writing, look at video and podcasts.

Your message needs a medium – it's up to you to consider which one or ones are best for you, your brand and your audience.

2. APPEARANCE

Attractive people are more well-liked and are seen to be more trustworthy. In one study, the conclusion was that the more attractive someone was, the higher the offer they received in a negotiation – even if they did not ask for more![17]

But here's the piece that I think gets lost in the discussion about appearance:

Everyone looks better on the outside when they feel good on the inside.

And while it might feel superficial, the more care and attention you take to look good on the outside, the better you will feel on the inside. Think about how good you feel after a great haircut or after a good workout. It's a circle that feeds itself.

A client working to raise money for his real estate portfolio commented that people didn't seem to take him seriously. When I asked him what he was wearing when he met with them, he said, *"What I always wear at work – jeans and a golf shirt."*

I asked, *"And what about on your feet?"*

"Running shoes."

I asked him: *"Is that what the successful investor in you wears?"*

The answer was 'no.' He then confessed that he had previously been in the habit of taking a lot more care with his appearance but he had let it slide in the last year or two.

After our conversation, he stopped wearing running shoes and jeans and started having more interesting conversations. By

---

17 Sara J. Solnick and Maurice E. Schweitzer, "The Influence of Physical Attractiveness and Gender on Ultimatum Game Decisions," *Organizational Behavior and Human Decision Processes* 79, no. 3 (Sept. 1999), 199-215.

dressing better, he felt better about himself. He was able to boldly step into conversations he'd previously shied away from.

Wear what makes *you* feel awesome and confident. Chances are you're not feeling that way in track pants and white runners. And you probably don't feel all that awesome if you're not on top of your hygiene either.

I want to emphasize, however, that this is not about designer name brands or suits – unless that is who you are. It's about dressing so you feel like your fabulous self.

Garrett Gee is a 25-year-old who sold his QR Code Scanning App to SnapChat for 54 million dollars. He wore skinny jeans, a T-shirt, and Adidas flip flops on the TV show *Shark Tank* and also when he had meetings with Google, Facebook and Lady Gaga.

It might sound like the outfit of someone who doesn't care, but he dressed with intention. He explained that these clothes were part of the 'uniform' he put together when raising money for the company. His intention was to ensure that his investors could see him for who he was – no pretense.[18] He felt comfortable and confident in those clothes.

In Silicon Valley where Mark Zuckerberg wears the same grey T-shirt almost every day,[19] it is not surprising to see someone dress so casually; it seems to be part of tech culture.

That may not be the best look for you, though. Go back to the words you want associated with you and your brand – and figure out what you will wear that makes you feel great and look great.

Most of us weren't born with supermodel looks, but you can make the most of what you've been given. And when you take care to *look* your best, check in with yourself: you will probably be feeling better on the inside too.

---

18 http://nextshark.com/garrett-gee-scan-bucket-list-family/
19 http://www.businessinsider.com/mark-zuckerberg-same-t-shirt-2014-11

If you're not sure where to start, ask your hairstylist if your hair style is the right one for your face shape. Ask your dentist about improving your smile. When you go shopping for clothes, consult with someone about what best suits your body type and lifestyle. Also, maintain a healthy body weight – it's good for your health, your attitude and your appearance.

Find a look that makes you *feel* like the successful person you are and that you know in your heart you're meant to be.

3. GOOGLE Results

It's not about having a website or a cleverly crafted logo, but as discussed in the last chapter, your brand will be impacted by what is coming up in the search engines about you, so it's an important part of the formula for your brand.

4. I AM an expert in (and what I am not an expert in)

Please don't get hung up on the word 'expert,' thinking you must be one before you begin building your brand. This is more about *choosing a niche and focusing*. By doing that, you will rapidly become an expert, but you don't have to start there before you build your brand.

When you focus on a smaller area, you can more easily attract the right people and avoid wasting time on the wrong people.

Some people resist focusing on a niche for fear there isn't enough to go around so they try to be everything to everybody, but then their positioning isn't clear.

The big mistake to avoid here is trying *to be everything to everyone*.

I see realtors make this mistake all the time. They claim to 'specialize' in an entire region that covers six different cities. As an investor in one city, I could barely keep up with everything that was happening in the three neighborhoods I focused on. There's no way you're truly an expert in six different cities! And, that's okay. People won't remember that you are a realtor for New York – covering Brooklyn, Queens and Manhattan, but they will remember the guy who specializes in loft style condos in the Meatpacking District of Manhattan.

To start, think about the single thing you want to be known for. You need to be known for *something*!

Pick a niche. Become well known in that niche and expand from there.

Remember: *"An expert is not someone who knows what he knows. An expert is someone who is **known** for knowing what he knows."*[20]

The bigger the subject, skill or geographical area you're trying to be an expert in, the more difficult it will be to become known as *the* expert. I love being Canadian for this reason – we're already starting with a smaller pool of people. But you still want to narrow down the niche that you're known for. I'd have a big battle to become known as *the* go-to expert in Canada on all things to do with 'influence.' But, there are a lot fewer people who can say they are *the* go-to expert on personal branding or selling for the non-sales person.

5. CHARACTER

Your character goes back to the idea of 'Who You Be.' What do you stand for? What can people expect from you?

Your values come through in how you do things. It's not *what* you do that matters as much as *how* you do it.

Your values aren't things you need to tell people about. They will know.

Taylor Swift's support of the underdog and appreciation for her fans is very deeply rooted in her brand.

She doesn't *tell* you she values these things – she *shows* it by doing amazing things to recognize her fans, and by standing up to big companies like Apple for the small artists who can't.

---

20 Tsufit, *Step into the Spotlight: A Guide to Getting Noticed,* Toronto, p. 12

You don't have to *say* you value workplace diversity if your company has people from all kinds of backgrounds working there.

If you always show up prepared and on time, people will know you respect them. You won't have to *tell* them.

It's about consciously choosing what values are important to you, so you can make sure this shines through in everything you do. When you are consistent, you don't have to tell people what you value; they will know.

Ask yourself:

- What values are important to me?

- What values do I want associated with me and my brand?

- Are you *doing* the things you need to do so that people associate those values with you and your brand?

Now you're starting to formulate a picture of your brand. The ultimate goal is to be chased, not chasing. Your brand is what will make people think of you when someone says, "Do you know anybody that can help with x?"

But your brand might not be doing that right now.

What makes someone chase you? You have something they want.

It seems simple, but humans aren't simple. Our brains don't want to work too hard, and our survival fears mean we run when chased, so your message has to be something we turn to, not run away from.

The art is in how you let other people know who you are and how you can help. Getting clear and implementing the Brand Magic Formula™ will help.

The approach is to offer *value* that demonstrates why you're the best person to work with, and to create a *brand* that says a lot about you without you ever opening your mouth.

If you feel like you have to *convince* someone to do something, then you've missed an important part of creating your brand and building your authority. Perhaps you're in front of the wrong person, or maybe your message is not clear, or maybe you've done something to lose their trust.

There's nothing more uncomfortable than the needy feeling that you *have* to get someone to do something. **Everything you're learning here is designed to entice the right people to step forward and *ask* to work with you or *ask* about buying your product.**

 KEY POINTS

- Start with who you are to develop your own 'Be. Do. Have.' goals.

- What words do you want people to associate with you? Make your list.

- The Brand Magic Formula™:

  1. Message

  2. Appearance

  3. Google Results

  4. I am an expert in...

  5. Character

CHAPTER 7

Listen To Me!

It was nothing I had planned to watch. I just happened to be near the TV when it started...

A young, professional looking woman is running down the sidewalk, checking her watch. She opens a large door to a bustling bar and looks around for someone.

When she thinks she finds him, she confirms that he's Harrison, and then without taking a breath she launches into a speech:

> *I can't stay ... I only came to tell you I can't stay. I didn't have your number and getting stood up at this particular bar is like falling face first on a runway.*

I can't stay is what I'm saying. I don't do blind dates.

She thinks it's a blind date.

It's not. It's a job interview.

Actually ... it's not even a job interview. It's a job *offer.*

Two minutes and eleven seconds. That's how far into the show it was when I knew I was hooked. I never meant to watch it, but it grabbed my attention with that opening scene. Had it not, I would have shut it off, gone to bed and never looked back. Instead, I have been a loyal fan of *Scandal*'s Olivia Pope and her team of gladiators in suits ever since.

Your opening scene with a prospect can't be boring, or they will switch channels and be gone ... not just for the day, but forever.

So how did Shonda Rhimes, creator of *Scandal* (and *Grey's Anatomy, How to Get Away with Murder,* etc.), know exactly how to hook me – and the other 7.33 million viewers[21] who tuned into that first episode – and keep us coming back for more? And bringing their friends ... Season 3 opened with over 10 million viewers!?

She did it the same way that you'll create intrigue, curiosity and engagement with your ideal customer....

First, Shonda knows her audience. She's proven with several hit shows that she knows *who* is watching her shows and *what* they want ... and she delivers.

Before you do *anything*, you have to understand who your audience is. The same thing that will intrigue me is *not* the same thing that will intrigue my 14-year-old niece, my 38-year-old carpenter brother, or my 98-year-old Grandma.

Fail to really understand who you're trying to influence, and you won't be able to hit the right emotional buttons to reel them in and hook them. We've talked about this already, but it's critical.

You also need to understand what they want, what they need and how they want to feel.

Dig deep into their *emotions* because that is how to really connect with them.

What are their desires and fears? What makes them laugh? What makes them cry?

That's where Shonda Rhime's magical powers of captivation work wonders. She knows how to grab and keep our attention.

---

21 That number is only US viewers ... so Shonda had a lot more people than 7.3 million people tuning in to her show. http://en.wikipedia.org/wiki/List_of_Scandal_episodes

She also has triggering tears down to a science (if you watch *Grey's Anatomy*, you know what I mean – watch without tissue at your own peril).

If you haven't made your audience curious enough to pay attention, you won't even get two minutes and eleven seconds.

Know your people so well that you can make them instantly curious and interested.

THE CROCODILE AT THE GATE

The brain has three parts: the neocortex, the limbic system, and the brain stem.

The neocortex is where we do our processing and higher level thinking; the limbic system is responsible for emotions; and the brain stem – also commonly called the croc brain – is in charge of our survival.

Going back to primitive days, the croc brain kept us alive. These days, where our survival isn't threatened constantly, it mostly protects our brain from having to work too hard. It acts like a gate and filters the vast amount of information coming at the brain to determine what we need to pay attention to.

It also makes us afraid of things that aren't actually life threatening.

The croc brain operates with a very simple filter. It looks at what is in front of it and determines:

1. *Can I eat it?* **Unless you're speaking to Hannibal Lecter, you're not a food option for the person you're speaking with, so this isn't how you'll gain attention for your personal brand.**

2. *Can I mate with it?* **If your goal is a phone number for a date, work this angle. It's not the one I'll suggest you focus on for your business though.**

- 3. *Is it dangerous?* **You're not going to be able to influence anyone that runs from you, so you need to avoid triggering any sort of fear or suspicion in the brain of the person you're speaking with or you'll lose him.**

- 4. *Is it new or interesting?* **If it's not, the brain is going to ignore it, so this is where you must focus your attention.**

What's going to grab the attention of the person you're speaking to? That's the key.

Oren Klaff, author of an excellent book called *Pitch Anything*, describes the croc brain as "a cognitive miser whose primary interest is survival. It doesn't like to do a lot of work and is high maintenance when it is forced to perform."[22]

He also cautions his readers regarding when they make a pitch to another person:

> We assume that our audience will do what we want them to do if our idea is good, if we didn't stumble through the pitch, and if we showed a winning personality. Turns out, it doesn't work that way. What is vitally important is making sure your message fulfills two objectives: First, you don't want your message to trigger fear alarms. And second, you want to make sure it gets recognized as something positive, unexpected, and out of the ordinary – a pleasant novelty.

This is not just useful to keep in mind for your business or when you're selling. Your brand needs to be positive, unexpected and out of the ordinary so you get noticed and remembered.

Casting Directors look for actors who are perfect for the part and who stand out. If you're an actor, like my husband Dave, your goal is to be new

22   Oren Klaff, *Pitch Anything.* Toronto: McGraw Hill, 2011), 15

and interesting even if you're playing an "every guy" kind of part. There has to be something about you that stands out so you're memorable.

If you learn to create curiosity and intrigue ... you learn how to get your audience to wonder where the nicely dressed woman is going and who she is looking for in the busy bar ... you succeed in passing the filter. Now you have to captivate them; you need to make them eager to know more.

Shonda Rhimes did this in Scandal with quick dialogue, the start of a story you need to know the ending to, and a character you (her ideal audience member) can instantly relate to in some way.

It all begins with knowing deeply who your audience is.

LAUGHTER LEADS TO LISTENING

Have you ever been to Mexico?

When you walk down a public space like a beach or a boardwalk, typically there are vendors everywhere – yelling to get your attention.

When you first arrive, you may start off politely saying "No, gracias." Soon though, you're ignoring them completely, until a man yells:

> *Hey lady! It's almost free! Come here – I want to sell you some stuff you don't need.*

You can't help but chuckle. You smile. You look over and see he actually has a lovely collection of hats or silver. Of course you really don't need anything, but he made you smile, and you let your guard down, and now you're at least looking at him whereas you've just ignored dozens of others.

If you can make someone laugh or even smile, they will be more open to hearing you, and your message is also a lot more likely to spread. When a flight attendant uses creativity when giving the safety message and someone catches it on video, it goes viral. Look up 'Southwest flight attendant safety message' or 'West Jet flight attendant funny safety message,' and you'll see a few videos with millions of views. The same old boring briefing that regular fliers completely ignore will get heard and even shared when it makes people smile.

Humor is tricky though. It is easy to get it wrong. If you're trying to make your spouse laugh, it's okay to miss with your jokes, but in a business setting you don't want the room to go silent because your joke offended someone or didn't make any sense.

The benefit of a good laugh often outweighs the risks so it's good to try to inject safe humor into what you do.

Robert Orben, professional comic and speech writer, said "When we laugh, we temporarily give ourselves over to the person who makes us laugh."[23]

That's pretty powerful, so it's worth trying, right?

THREE TIPS FOR GETTING BUSINESS-APPROPRIATE LAUGHS

1. Don't take yourself too seriously

The line, *"I used to think it was weird that dogs had nipples on their stomach ... then I looked at myself naked"* might work for a stand-up comic like Judy Carter, but for most of us, that's a visual we'd rather not have associated with our brand, right?

Putting yourself down, ridiculing religion and race, and profuse swearing are common in stand-up comedy, but not appropriate for *most* business brands. There are exceptions, of course, but it's not going to work unless that is just you being raw and open and it connects with your audience.

---

23 Mel Helitzer. *Comedy Writing Secrets*. (Cincinatti: Writers Digest Books, 2005, 11.

Your goal is to make your ideal client feel comfortable and connect with you in a positive way. You can do this really well by getting a laugh, but it has to be a laugh for the right reasons.

My suggestion is to show your human side – the side that we all can relate to – in a way that gets a laugh.

The best approach is to share something that illustrates that you are just like your audience. We all have unique experiences or mindless moments that can get a chuckle from the audience. Being so nervous that I forgot to put pants on is an example of something I've done. When our friend Guillermo was new to Canada, he went to a party where Diana Krall was a guest. When he shook hands with her, he said "Nice to meet you. And what do you do?" He said he immediately knew something was off when he asked that, because he could feel people watching them, but she humbly replied, "I sing."

He was encouraging, saying "Oh that's so good!" She mentioned that she had just been singing in Argentina, where he was from. He smiled, picturing her performing at small clubs, and said, "Wonderful! Where did you visit?"

His jaw dropped when she casually replied that she'd been performing at the Gran Teatro Rex, which is a major venue in Buenos Aries. He later found out how well known she is, and how beloved she is in the city of Nanaimo, where the party was. He felt a bit embarrassed, but it was an innocent conversation and it makes for a great story. He had everyone's attention at the Christmas party where he was telling the story. Nobody burst into hilarious laughter but we all chuckled at what had happened. That's all you need.

Have fun with the things that happen to you or the thoughts you have. Jerry Seinfeld does this well in his stand-up comedy acts. "I like tiny hotel soap; I pretend that it's normal soap and my muscles are huge," and "You know you're getting old when you get that one candle on the cake. It's like 'See if you can blow this out.'"

Make a note of it when funny things happen. You can leave yourself a voice memo on your phone, send yourself an email, or just keep a little notebook handy where you jot down everyday things that are amusing. You think you'll remember, but you might not, so write it down. You never know when it could be a great story or idea for something you can use in your talks, marketing or everyday conversations.

2. Kid humor

Kids don't have the same filter that adults do and this makes for some great stories. A child will say it like it is, and that can be really funny.

You know ... when you say, "I love you sweetie" to your daughter and she says, "I love me too!" Or, "I took my son to the doctor and he had to pee in a cup. After he finished, he looked at me and said, 'You're not going to make me drink it, are you?'"

Kid humor is usually pretty safe and if it can fit in with a conversation or a talk, it will likely get a laugh.

3. An unexpected twist

When someone expects a certain response, shake them out of their default mode by surprising them. My Dad is good at this. When you ask him "How are you?" he responds with "Charming."

When you ask him "What are you up to?" he might say, "About 5'8' and 185 pounds but I'm trying to lose weight."

That's how he gets attention and starts conversations. It works well for disarming people and being remembered. A simple way of going for the unexpected is what Jerry Corley, in his Comedy Clinic, calls a 'cliché reformation.' Look for things commonly said in your business, evaluate its intended meaning, and come up with a comedic meaning.

For example:

Never give up on your dreams. Keep sleeping.

To uncover these kinds of opportunities to add humor, look at common clichés or sayings for your industry. Ask yourself:

- What is assumed?

- Is there a double entendre? In other words, what could it mean that it's not intended to mean?

- Are there two dissimilar ideas converging?

The book *Comedy Writing Secrets* has eight chapters on humor writing techniques and dedicates three chapters to this type of 'Play on Words' technique because it is so powerful. The author, Mel Helitzer, defines a Play on Words as "a twist on a familiar cliché; aphorism; book, movie, or song title; famous quote; national ad slogan – in fact, any expression widely known by the public. It can make use of double entendres, homonyms, or puns."

It's an unexpected response.

Whenever somebody expects something and you can deliver something different, you'll get attention. Using this technique in your communications now and again will definitely make people keep reading, listening and engaging with you.

> *If Apple made a car would they put in Windows?*
>
> *I'd like to tell you some jokes about unemployed people, but I won't. None of them work.*
>
> *If at first you don't succeed, then sky diving isn't for you.*[24]

Humor is a powerful tool. Used in just the right way, it can be the perfect opening to gain attention and connect with your client, ease tension in a meeting, or build rapport with your audience.

---

24 Mel Helitzer, *Comedy Writing Secrets* (USA: Writers Digest Books, 2005), 106.

IS YOUR VOICE RUINING YOUR CREDIBILITY?

My friend Katie has a giant white dog named Bossco. He loves to swim in the lake and fetch a ball. But, when he brings it back to you he tries to play tug with it. He weighs more than 100 pounds! You're not going to win *any* game of tug with him, and certainly not a game where you're trying to hold onto the side of a tennis ball.

You have to give him the command 'leave it' so he will drop it.

The problem? The words aren't enough. You have to say 'leave it' in a deep, gruff, firm voice. Then, like magic, the ball drops out of his mouth, and his tail wags happily while he waits for you to throw it again.

It's not just dogs that respond to lower voices. Voice pitch impacts the selection of leaders and our social perception of each other. Both men and women prefer lower pitched voices in leaders. In research on gender roles, leadership is seen as a masculine role. But even *more* interesting is that people associate traits like integrity, strength and competence with a lower pitched voice. Based on voice pitch alone, someone may instantly consider you competent and trustworthy![25]

A study by Duke University's Fuqua School of Business found that male CEO's with lower-pitched voices were more likely to manage larger companies, made up to $187,000 more in annual income, and were more likely to enjoy a tenure of up to five months longer in that role.[26]

Low voices matter in Hollywood too! The movie *In a World* is all about a woman who wants to do the voice-over for movie trailers. She's competing against deep-voiced men, like her father, for the coveted roles. It's a great example of the bias in our society towards lower-pitched voices.

---

25 Rindy C. Anderson and Casey A. Klofstad, *Preference for Leaders with Masculine Voices Holds in the Leadership Roles.* Published: December 12, 2012. PLOS One. DOI: 10.1371/journal.pone.0051216.

26 Robert Lee Hotz, "How to Train Your Voice to Be More Charismatic," *The Wall Street Journal, Health and Wellness* (December 1, 2015).

No worries if your voice isn't the perfect low pitch. Yes, if you sound like a squeaky toy, you may wish to work with a vocal coach to lower your natural pitch a bit, but there are a lot of other things you can work on with your voice in order to impact how your message is heard and respected.

THERE'S MORE TO YOUR VOICE THAN VOCAL PITCH

"It's really simple. These are the factors we have to put in the model...." And then my classmate would rapidly rattle off a list of things, but none of us ever knew exactly what he'd said.

We were completing a group project for one of our MBA classes. This guy had a gift for numbers and a work ethic that ensured he'd be top of the class even without his big brain.

The problem was, as a group, we often didn't understand what he was saying. His words came out rapid fire.

Most of the time we just followed his lead, but problems arose when there was a question about what we should do. He spoke so rapidly that his arguments weren't compelling. Our group often hit stalemates, unsure of what to do; and as a result, our project got a B – a grade he was not used to seeing on his transcripts.

Your voice – the pace you speak at, the tone you use to communicate, filler words, and the energy that comes through in your voice – are all impacting your ability to influence and impress other people.

A quick look back at some of the most famous Seinfeld episodes will confirm the importance of how you deliver your message. They've had fun with the fast talker, the close talker, and the low talker.

Remember, how Jerry was 'low talked' into wearing that white puffy pirate shirt on stage at his show by Kramer's low talking girlfriend?

Clearly, *how* you're delivering your message is critical. So what can you do to ensure your message has the greatest impact on delivery? Here are a few thoughts:

WHERE DOES YOUR VOICE COME FROM?

Video –
3 Ways Your
Voice is Ruining
Your Credibility
https://youtu.be/
cOgAKmlHa08

When I was an employee selling real estate data for a company called RealNet, there was one type of prospect that I often had trouble selling, and that was the small builder or developer. These companies didn't have an analyst on staff like the larger companies did, so they didn't have the capacity to process raw data efficiently; and they typically had only one development project on the go at a time.

The data was useful to them but they wanted it in a simple report with information that was specific to their area only.

But that was not what we offered. We offered an annual subscription service that gave them access to a ton of raw data for the whole region.

My boss, the owner and founder of the company, enthusiastically pumped me up before these sales calls. He believed these companies would make better decisions with this data; and they would. The problem wasn't the data. The problem was that the format and delivery of the data didn't suit these guys.

Not surprisingly, in my first year, I made 10 to 15 sales calls to prospects like this and only closed one of them. The one I closed also asked me out on a date after they signed up (I politely declined) and promptly cancelled their subscription when the contract was up for renewal.

When it came to selling this product to larger builders and developers who had an analyst in-house to do the work for them, and had multiple projects going on at any one time, the sales call was easier and my success rate was higher.

The fit was better, but I think the bigger factor in my success with the larger companies was that I believed it was the right solution for their business.

Maybe I was wrong, but I believed we didn't have the right solution for the smaller guys, and as a result I sold almost nothing to them.

TRYING TO CONVINCE SOMEBODY OF SOMETHING YOU DON'T BELIEVE IN?

How is it working for you?

It's a bit like the word association exercise from my friend Scott Bell that we covered earlier. If you believe that most salespeople are slimy, you're going to struggle to sell anything.

What you believe matters. It comes through in how you are delivering your message even if you aren't aware of it (and you rarely are).

If you try to be something you're not, people will sense it, even if they can't quite put their finger on it, because you won't be in alignment with what you're presenting.

The first key to having an influential brand and an impactful presentation is to *believe* what you're saying.

I watched an excellent interview between Oren Klaff, author of *Pitch Anything*, and a professional interrogator (aka an international spy) Simon Treselyan.[27]

In turning assets or interrogating terrorists, Simon had to get information as quickly as possible. To do that without force, he explained, he'd have to get into an emotional state where he really was interested in what the person had to say and how he could be of service to them. He said as

---

27 Watch the interview here: http://pitchanything.com/done-deal-with-simon-treselyan/

soon as someone senses you have structure to your questioning, they get defensive, you lose rapport, and you will not get any information.

I think this is a great way to describe what happens to a lot of people when they try to sell something. They are comfortable and having a good conversation, right up until they have to ask somebody for the business, and then they get all weird. Their sales training kicks in and they try to ask 'test close' questions and move to the formal close, but then everything falls apart.

If you truly *believe in* what you offer, that will come through when you speak. Learn how to present what you have to offer in an enticing and interesting way, but ultimately, let the belief in *what you do and how you can help them* carry you through your conversation. It's not about a perfect presentation; it's about getting into a *state* where the needs of the person you're speaking with are *important* to you, and you *want* to help them.

ARE YOU COMMITTED?

In Grant Cardone's book, *The 10X Rule,* he talks about the danger of not being fully committed to whatever it takes to achieve your goal.

He says:

> *"When you have underestimated the time, energy, and effort necessary to do something, you will have 'quit' in your mind, voice, posture, face and presentation.... However, when you correctly estimate the effort necessary, you will assume the appropriate posture. The marketplace will sense by your actions that you are a force to be reckoned with and are not going away – and it will begin to respond accordingly."*[28]

Belief and determination will shine through in your voice.

Are you 'trying' to get something done, or are you 'getting' it done?

---

28 Grant Cardone, *The 10x Rule: The Only Difference Between Success and Failure.* (New Jersey: John Wiley & Sons Inc., 2011), 15.

Whether you say it one way or another won't matter nearly as much as what you believe is true.

When I called my husband from King Street in Toronto the day I decided to quit my job, he didn't question it at all. He just said, "Okay – well, we'll figure it out."

I was earning the majority of our household income at the time. It wasn't a small thing that I was quitting and I didn't have a real plan in place to earn money.

He would have questioned me if he thought I had doubts. He would have tried to talk me out of it if he hadn't sensed my own certainty.

My conviction that it was something I had to do and that I was going to find a way to make it work came through without me saying those words.

Get connected with what is driving you to create your brand and to have an impact and influence others. Get into the mindset of 'whatever it takes' and pursue what you want with moxie.

That kind of fire inside you will be burning so bright in your brand that you'll erase many of the potential 'voice issues' that can come up.

RECORD YOURSELF SPEAKING

If you just groaned at the thought of recording yourself speaking, I get it. Listening to your own voice can be pretty painful.

But, your voice could be costing you money!

Listening to your side of a business call is the best way to find out if you have any of those other potential voice issues that are making it hard for you to influence others.

Listen for:

1. **Vocal Tone** – Does your voice come through as a command or a question? If your voice inflects up at the end of your sentences, people are going to hear questions instead of statements, which can make them doubt if you know what you're talking about. Ideally, at the end of an important sentence, drop your voice down a bit. That will come through as a confident command.

2. **Filler Words** –Of course you already know that you should avoid 'um' and 'ah' when you speak, but there are a lot of other words we lean on to fill empty spaces. My latest word is 'right?' Sounds innocent enough, but in listening to one of my training sessions, I caught myself using it way too much. It was distracting.

   Filler words distract people if they come up more than a few times. They can also dramatically reduce your credibility. You may even find they are making you sound younger or older than you want to sound. *The Globe and Mail* reported a new initiative by the Edwards School of Business at the University of Saskatchewan *to eliminate filler words*. The Dean began the effort because she heard 'like, you know' all over the halls. Interestingly, it was pointed out to her that she used words that made her sound old to the students, including 'well,' 'look,' 'I mean,' and 'basically.' [29]

   Have a listen to find what your favorite filler words are and make an effort to get rid of them. You will sound more confident and credible, and your message will

---

29 http://www.theglobeandmail.com/report-on-business/careers/business-education/b-school-competition-forbids-like-you-know-filler-words/article27713673

have a lot more impact. What to do instead? Try taking a pause instead of adding in a space-filling word.

3. **Vocal Pace** – Too fast, too slow, too monotone. We covered why 'too fast' is challenging. 'Too slow' is often associated with a lack of intelligence; and 'too monotone'—well, it puts people to sleep. Change it up. Personally, I prefer people who slow down for key points and talk quickly (but not too quickly) for everything else. Tell me your stories with varied voice tones and a varied pace. By recording yourself, you'll hear where you may want to make changes.

Think this isn't that important? At the end of a workshop that we ran, a woman came up to me and said, "I can't believe I am doing it!"

She went on explain that she had been in the same job for eight years and had been passed over for a promotion three times. The most recent time she had been absolutely stunned because she had far more experience and was more qualified for the position than the person they promoted. When she asked why she wasn't chosen, her boss said, *"People don't think you know what you're talking about."*

She had no idea why that was the case, or what she could do to resolve the issue, until she was in our workshop. While working with her partner on a practice sales pitch, her partner let her know that most of her sentences ended with her voice going *higher*.

Instead of giving her team commands or stating her opinion, it sounded like she was *asking a question*.

 Read the following sentence out loud three ways. First, read it without allowing your voice to change tone at all. Then at the end, raise your voice up for the last two words. And finally, drop your voice down for the last two words:

This is the course of action we need to take.

You should be able to hear that the second version, where your voice tone rises, sounds like you are doubtful and unsure. The third version comes through with authority; it's a command.

Of course you have your own personal communication style, and this is *not* about being someone you're not. This is about having a higher level of awareness of what you do and how others may perceive you as a result. When you're aware, you can choose to change if you want to have a different impact.

I was on a webinar yesterday with a guy who said, first thing, *"I talk really fast. You can go ahead and ask me to slow down, but I am telling you now I am just going to tell you to listen faster."*

He could change his presentation style, but he has chosen not to. But he acknowledges this to the audience so they know that he's aware and that this is who he is. That kind of confidence and authority can work too.

 ## KEY ACTION ITEMS:

- Know your people so well you can make them instantly curious about your message.

- Laughter leads to listening, so bring humor into your messages as often as possible.

- Build your own belief into your message so it comes through in your voice.

- Record yourself speaking and listen for vocal tone issues, filler words, and your vocal pace to ensure your voice is not ruining your credibility.

CHAPTER 8

What's Your Story?

When you think about what you're going to eat for dinner, you probably aren't thinking, "Okay, a salad with feta cheese, no dressing, apples and kale has 420 calories, 3 grams of protein, and 7 grams of carbs. The allocation for the day is 2,000 calories, so after the 1220 calories I've already consumed, that leaves me with a few hundred calories for a glass of wine and a piece of dark chocolate."

You're probably thinking, "Crap. My doctor said I shouldn't eat so much red meat, so I guess I'll eat that kale salad that's in the fridge. Salad is so much work to chew though, so boring. Oh! But I do have that bottle of red wine from the dinner party on Saturday, so that will be perfect, with a piece of dark chocolate – a reward for being so good about eating the Kale salad. Okay, this will be great. "

Our mind will process data, but in processing the data we look for the how and the why. We create a story about the data to understand it.

It's why the quote "Statistics are used much like a drunk uses a lamp-post ... more for support than illumination" really is true. We use stats to *back up* our viewpoint; rarely do we use stats and facts to *create* our viewpoint.

A STORY WILL MAKE SENSE OUT OF LIFE IN A WAY THAT NOTHING ELSE DOES.

Building good stories into what you do is important because people love to consume stories and they are incredibly powerful for influencing.

Plus, by giving your audience a story, you increase the chance that you have an impact on the story *they* tell about *you*. Because that is the most important story of all ... the one that is told about *you* when you leave the room.

Annette Simmons, author of *The Story Factor*, says "Telling a meaningful story means inspiring your listeners – coworkers, leaders, subordinates, family, or a bunch of strangers – to reach the same conclusions you have reached and *decide for themselves* to believe what you say and do what you want them to do."[30]

You'll always want to work on developing new stories. To begin, develop four key stories that you'll use to:

- Get people interested and excited about what you do
- Explain why you do it
- Handle (or even better, block) objections
- Influence your customer to take action so they can live a better life/solve their problem.

Some of my coaching clients hear this message and just start telling stories. Then they wonder why their stories aren't working.

When you tell a story, make sure you know the reason *why* you're telling that story. What do you hope someone will say, do or think after you tell them your story?

Tell stories with a clear intent. Are you trying to build credibility or create curiosity? Perhaps you want to open the door to a potential opportunity. Or maybe you want to block a common objection from coming up.

A story I might share would be about my client who wanted to land his first big 'done-for-you package' client. This was a $25,000 package – substantially more than he'd ever charged for anything before. He

---

30 Annette Simmons, *The Story Factor: Secrets of Influence from the Art of Storytelling.* (New York: Basic Books, 2006), 17.

had his first lead for a potential client and was pretty nervous about it.

He carefully crafted an email to land the client and sent it to me to get my thoughts on how he was presenting the options.

I sent him back a single line: "Don't email this! Email him *only* to get an appointment to speak. I'll tell you what to say once you have the appointment!"

My client trashed that email, booked an appointment, and I walked him through how to have the conversation. He needed to first understand what was most important to his potential client. Assuming my client could deliver everything this person wanted, my client could then present the options, framing the done-for-you package exactly as this person wanted.

Immediately after his call with the prospect, my client emailed me: "*I was totally wrong about what his goals were for this project! I would have blown it with my first email! I can't believe how well that worked. I could have charged even more! Thank you!*"

That story tells you a little bit about how I help, and it lets you know that when you make an offer, it should always be in terms of what is most important to your potential client – or you could lose the sale.

There are an endless number of stories you *could* tell. Some will have more drama and excitement. Some will have humor. But all will have the purpose of communicating an important message to your audience.

Make sure you know why you're telling the story you're telling.

To do that, you need to think about the stories and your desired impact in advance.

A few stories you should work on creating include:

- **Your genesis story** – Whatever business you are in, you have a genesis story. But you may not have spent any time developing it.

Now is your chance to do that.

"I knew I could make money doing this" is not a story that has impact. Maybe that is partially true, but I hope there's a deeper reason why you're doing what you're doing.

Ultimately, this story is the answer to the question: **How did you get into that?**

When you write a book, there are a couple of questions you'll be asked. One of them is: "Why did you write this book?"

Any media interviews I did for my first book, *More than Cashflow,* always included that question.

Depending on the situation and the amount of time available, the story would vary, but the typical answer was something like this:

> *When we first started investing in real estate, we made some pretty big mistakes. The worst one resulted in us being the owners of a crack house. We'd taken courses to learn how to invest, but the instructors glossed over the risks and made it all sound quick and easy. And it wasn't just **us** making mistakes … many others were struggling as investors after being sold by the big promises. We found that most books and courses talked about how to make money, but none really shared what could go wrong, or how to make the best decisions for your lifestyle.*
>
> *I then realized that there was a definite need to share some real-life stories of the good **and** the bad so people could actually use real estate to create the life they wanted … if they were still up for it after they learned about the real risks.*

That's my genesis story for why I wrote my first book. To help you create your genesis story, think about these three questions:

1. Why did you get into your field?

2. How did you first see or experience the problem or issue that led you to start your business / create the product / write the book?

3. What is the desired outcome that drives you to do what you do?

- **Before-and-after stories** – You can read minds. Or at least it will feel that way when you get these stories right. It might include your own before-and-after story, but the more stories that cover where a client was *before* working with you, the better. The story will typically cover their fears, their challenges, what their situation was, and how it worked out in the end. Some common situations to consider:

    > *Want to make a change but are hesitating.* For example, if you offer a nutritional plan for clients, some may hesitate because of the added expense or the time it will take to prepare meals. Or they might fear that they will never get to eat bread again. Do you have a story of someone else that had this concern and then got results, and even found they saved money because they hadn't realized the cost of that coffee and cookie snack every afternoon? Or how they got results and were still able to enjoy their favorite treat when the craving called?

    > *Are afraid they will make the wrong decision.* This can be a fable that addresses the fact that *no choice* is a decision all on its own. It could be a story of a client that *didn't* act and then suffered until they finally came back to work with you. Or, it could just be a story that will reassure them that the decision to work with you is one that they will be happy with, that their family will approve of, and that others will be envious of.

    > *Want to look good to their friends, family and coworkers.* A common objection you might hear is: 'I have to talk with

my wife.' That may be true, but the bigger concern on their mind is what their buddies on the hockey team, their father-in-law, or their nosy neighbor will say about the purchase.

We all have a mental rolodex of people we 'consult with' before we make a decision[31]. Rarely do we *actually* consult with these people, but we mentally check in to consider what certain people would say or think about our decision.

The challenge is that many people don't understand themselves well enough to really know what their true concern is. That means it's up to *you* to know your ideal client well enough to figure out who in their life they will think about when they make a decision about whether to work with you or not.

Find stories that will set their mind at ease and assure them that the important people in their life will be pumped that they made the right choice, and that they will look good in the eyes of others because of the decision they have made.

> *Are worried about how they will make money, save money or be financially secure in retirement.* People with a lot of money worry about keeping it, investing it, and even spending it. People with little money worry about keeping it, investing it and spending it.

When we were raising money for our deals, our ideal investor would tell us they wanted to generate a great return – grow their wealth and save for their retirement – without having to do any work. That was partially true but the real truth was that they were more worried about losing their money.

---

31 Kevin Hogan explains this concept in more detail here: https://youtu.be/6wefN4pD1SQ

It is very important to have stories that address both the fear that they are talking about and the actual fear.

- **Credibility stories**: These are stories that can demonstrate your authority, status and expertise without you saying it directly. Being humble about your achievements is typically viewed as a positive trait, but if you don't tell people what you do that is great, then people won't *know*. So this kind of story can let people know cool things about you, without coming across as bragging.

The context of the story, who else is in the story, the words that other people say, and what you do in a particular situation, all speak volumes about who you are.

Years ago, we were at an event that our friend and former business mentor Greg Habstritt put on in Calgary; it was called 'Engage Today.' He attracted some of the greatest speakers in North America to the event because Richard Branson was the guest of honor. Most people speaking at the event didn't even get to shake hands with Richard Branson, let alone speak with him, but they could now say 'they had shared the stage with Richard Branson.' And the stories they could tell about being a speaker at that event would give them instant credibility.

It really is that simple.

Speaking at a quarterly event put on by my friends Nick and Tom Karadza of Rock Star Real Estate, I was struck by how much they had grown. This event had 480 people in the room for a full day session! I knew how hard they had been working, but it was definitely paying off! They were even on *Profit Magazine's* list of the Top 500 Fastest Growing Companies in Canada in 2015.

I was telling Nick how cool it was to see their success. He replied, "It's funny you say that because when *you* were on stage, I was thinking about how much you've achieved too! Your book went to #1 overall on Amazon – how many people can say that? And you self-published! And our audience loved your talk – as usual."

His words of praise may have gone to my head though, because I left my laptop behind and didn't realize it until I was at the airport checking in to my flight! Thankfully a friend was close by and was able to grab the bag and get it to me before I had to board the plane!

In that quick story, you learned that I spoke in front of an audience of 480, that my book went to #1, and that my talk was a hit. I didn't say how great I was, but Nick did.

It's not a perfect story, but your stories don't have to be perfect to say a lot about you.

- **Stories that make people laugh**: Some stories you tell should be funny. As we already discussed, there's a lot of ways you can get people to laugh, and having some funny stories on hand is one of them. Your story may teach a lesson or be for another purpose besides laughter, but you want people to at least chuckle from time to time. Laughter leads to listening.

  Watch the best professional speakers and you'll notice they all have a lot of humor in their talks. In fact, some are more comedy than content, but that's often what audiences want.

There are other stories you will want to collect and have on hand as well, and once you get good at telling them, you'll be a much more powerful persuader than others who rely on facts and explanations.

HOW TO TELL A STORY

> *"You may have the insight of a Buddha, but if you cannot tell a story, your ideas turn dry as chalk."*
>
> Robert McKee

Story is powerful. We learn through story. Our history has been passed on through story.

Children are taught legends and fables so they learn key life lessons. Think of the stories you know from your childhood. One that I grew up with was the story of the Tortoise and the Hare. Slow and steady wins the race is something I often think of. Then there's the story of the boy who cried wolf, and the story of the goose who laid the golden egg. Through fables, we learn many lessons that last a lifetime.

But how do *you* create a memorable story or use one in your brand? Yes, you can use fables, but the most powerful stories are ones from *your* life, *your* business or *your* clients.

Some people are born storytellers; they have the gift of being able to grab your attention, bring little details to life, and keep you engaged from start to finish. But for those of us who are not born with this particular gift, it's necessary to hone our skills so we can tell stories that engage and connect with people.

Most stories, sadly, are boring. But even worse than being boring is that many stories have absolutely no purpose. Maybe the storyteller likes telling the story, but it has nothing to do with the listener.

A great story is actually fairly complex. There is context and subjectivity to stories. What makes a great story for one audience doesn't mean it's a universally great story. As a speaker, I can give the same talk at five different events and have five different reactions.

There are stories that will hit home with some people and not others. There are stories that will mean a lot more when they're in the context of something that is highly newsworthy at the time. Or in the context of something everyone in the room will understand or relate to.

Recently I heard Chris Hadfield, a great Canadian astronaut, speak. As a test pilot, and someone who has made three trips to space, he has a deep understanding of flying. To explain the risks of launching a rocket ship into space, he could have shared a bunch of technical details that would mean nothing to the layman. Instead, he said there are many things that can happen in a rocket launch that can end in catastrophe, and that the odds were one in 32 that something would go fatally wrong during a rocket launch. To put this in a context that meant something to us, he said: *"If Air Canada had the same odds, there would be nine fatal crashes every day!"*

You always need to know the audience that you're communicating with. In a room of rocket scientists, the risks of a rocket launch would be explained differently than in a room of business people in a small community.

While many of us may not be naturally talented storytellers, we can improve our storytelling ability if we keep in mind a few key principles.

LESSONS FROM THE GREAT ROBERT McKEE ON TELLING A STORY

Sitting in the back of a large hotel conference room, I watched this white-haired man shuffle up to the stage carrying a leather bag. He wore running shoes, dress pants, and a blue, long-sleeved shirt with a button-up collar; and it seemed like a strain for him to climb up the stairs and get settled on the stage.

"Wow – I guess that's Robert McKee! Can he make it through four days of this?!" I thought.

At 8:59 a.m. he took his watch off his wrist and placed it on the podium in front of him. He then turned his attention to the audience.

He stood tall, and with a sparkle in his eye he began: *"There's no smog in LA. It's just the stench of all the rotten scripts."*

Robert McKee is a Fulbright scholar and probably the best known screenwriting trainer and lecturer in the world. His students include hundreds of Emmy, Academy Award and Writers Guild Award winners.

When his 'Story Seminar' kicks off, he comes to life. This is a man who *lives* to teach about story telling.

Those four days of Robert McKee's seminar contained golden material to help with storytelling in life and in business.

Following are some of the great takeaways from the seminar. They will help you to get the attention of your audience, hold it, and make a big impact with your marketing messages.

NUMBERS KILL THOUGHT

Hearing about millions starving doesn't move us to donate as much as the plight of one single girl can.

Why is that? Certainly, a small girl is an identifiable victim. But, researchers state that it is because statistics make donors think analytically instead of emotionally. When you're thinking analytically, you will be less emotionally connected to the cause, and therefore you'll give less money.

To prove this, they ran a study asking one group analytical questions like: "If an object travels at five feet per minute, then by your calculations, how many feet will it travel in 360 seconds?" They asked the other group emotional questions, like: "Describe how you feel when you hear the word 'baby.'"

Then they gave both groups a letter that pleaded for help for a young girl named Rokia (a letter they'd originally used in tests to see the results of a plea for millions of people starving versus Rokia and her family starving).

When people were put in a more analytical mindset they gave $1.26. When they were set up to feel more emotional, they gave $2.34.[32]

Simply asking someone *one* analytical question caused a major *decrease* in support for the cause.

Robert McKee summarizes this by saying "numbers kill thought." The way we've been taught to present in business, with charts, graphs, and stats to back up our argument, is not a compelling way to connect with your audience and get buy-in.

A compelling story that illustrates the problem and your solution will connect your audience to you and to your message.

---

32 Dan and Chip Heath, *Made to Stick* (London: Arrow Books, 2008).

STORY MATTERS – BUT IT'S NOT THE STORY YOU THINK

It's easy to get hung up on the story you are telling. You want it to persuade, inspire and impact the person who hears it.

However, the story *you* tell is not the most important story.

The story that matters is the story *your client* (or potential client) tells after you leave the room.

That story will determine if you get the business and if your message made its mark.

So, you must give your client a story to pass along. This will be one of the four story types we've already covered. It might be your genesis story about how you helped someone just like them, or something related to your business that builds your credibility or gets a laugh.

Make it easy for someone to retell your story by giving singular and powerful revelations. It's not about information; it's about *insight*. Give them a cool perspective they can't wait to share.

Be specific. Too many confusing details or vague information, and the message will get diluted and eventually lost. Use concrete images they can visualize. Did he walk, or did he strut, or did he plod? Your mind actually *sees* the difference. Was it very big, or was it monstrous, gigantic, or towering three feet above your head?

 # TIP

If you're not sure whether your story is good, tell it to someone, and then ask them to repeat it back to you a few hours or a few days later. What details did they remember? What did they forget? Did they remember the important message? If they didn't, go back to your story and make some changes to the pieces they missed.

THE STORY YOU TELL IS NOT A NARRATIVE

A narrative walks you through someone's day, step by step. This morning I woke up to the sound of pounding rain. The storm had hit us hard overnight and I wondered if the gutters were overflowing. I looked at the clock; it was 5:55 a.m. My alarm was due to go off at 6:15, so I figured I'd get up so my husband wouldn't be disturbed by the alarm. I turned the alarm off and dressed in the dark.

That's a narrative. A story *can* be a narrative, but not all narratives are stories.

Whether you're producing a commercial, writing sales copy, or selling face to face, you want short stories with a big impact. To do that, your story should, for the most part, be a single point in time, with one key point that fuses emotion and mind.

Think of the classic comedian line: "So I'm standing there and...." So begins a single-point-in-time story that usually ends with you laughing.

Good stories don't have to be long. Here are some scary stories that are only two sentences long:

- We were sitting in the dark at the gym waiting for the power to come back on when my friend Breanne asked me why I was breathing so heavily. I wasn't.

- The laughter of a baby always makes you smile, doesn't it? Well, it does, unless it's 1 a.m. and you're home alone.

- With two dogs in the house, I am used to hearing scratching at the door. The problem is that I'm alone in a hotel room and I'm hearing scratching.

You'll probably tell a slightly longer story in most situations, but if you stick to a single point in time, you'll avoid the boring narrative.

CREATE A GOD-LIKE KNOWLEDGE OF THE SUBJECT

If you tell a story about a one-night stand that leads to pregnancy and it happens in the 21st century in the United States, you have a movie like *Knocked Up*. If you tell that story and it happens during the 1990's in Ireland, you get *The Snapper*. Even though the premise of the story is the same (a drunken hook-up), the entire story changes based on a few details like when and where it happened.

In an effort to make your message short, you will leave out some of the details, but you need certain pieces of information to bring your story to life. To know what details to leave out and which ones to include, you need to do a lot of research.

According to Robert McKee, in order to know what details are important to include or leave out, you need to create a 'god-like knowledge' of the subject. In business, knowing your industry is obviously important, as is a deep understanding of your competition. But knowing everything you can about your customers is probably the *most* important. Spend time speaking with your customers, observing them, reading what they read, and researching anything in detail that you don't quite understand or feel knowledgeable about.

With that depth of expertise, your specific stories will be easy for your ideal customers to relate to.

THE ENERGY COMES FROM THE NEGATIVE

The scene opens with the happy couple having coffee together. Everything is going well until a text message from her ex-boyfriend comes in. Now, the new boyfriend gets jealous and mad. He accuses her of leading her ex on. She gets up and leaves. The story doesn't get interesting until there's a negative energy.

If all you know about my first self-published book, *More than Cashflow*, is that thousands of copies were sold in the first week and that it went to #1 overall on Amazon in Canada, it's not very meaningful. It's not interesting until you hear about some of the obstacles I overcame, one big one being that I was turned down by the main publisher for this kind of book in Canada, because the marketing department didn't think my platform was good enough to sell any books. Basically, it wasn't my book idea that they rejected; they rejected *me*. They didn't think I would be able to sell a book.

Even if you've never wanted to be published, you've been rejected in some way at some point in your life. *That's* the part that you can relate to.

Bad things happen in business. There are challenges. Your story gets energy from the negative, so you *must* include it in the stories you tell, especially in business settings.

Story is a critical part of business success. The best leaders are almost always the best storytellers; they sell their vision through story, not stats.

Resist the urge to drown people in stats or platitudes, and get to the heart of what matters most in your business with a great story.

I will also note that I shouldn't have worried about whether Robert McKee could make it through his four-day seminar. Instead, I should have been wondering if *I* would be able to keep up with this 75-year-old man. His seminar was intense and inspiring. As long as people want to hear his lessons on story, Robert McKee will be out there sharing them. This is what he lives for. That's pretty cool.

5 TIPS TO HELP YOU CREATE A GREAT BRAND STORY

Take a look at the following starting lines from famous movies or books. Do you recognize where they came from?

> *"As far back as I can remember, I always wanted to be a gangster.[33]"*

---

33 Henry Hill (Ray Liotta) in *Goodfellas*.

"We were somewhere around Barstow on the edge of the desert when the drugs began to take hold.[34]"

"People are always asking me if I know Tyler Durden...[35]"

What do you notice about them? These classic examples all have five things in common ... five things you'll want to bring into the stories you tell for your brand and your business.

1. **Start in the middle of the action.**

   The traditional fairy tale starts with 'Once upon a time' but even then you find yourself in the middle of a situation. The princess is trapped in a tower, the prince can't find a suitable wife, or the peasant girl dreams of living a better life. The examples above all throw you right into it the middle of what is happening and it grabs you.

   Pay close attention to the next movie you watch. Movies usually dive right into a moment where something interesting is happening. The background story will be built in later, but the opening grabs your attention.

2. **Tell the story from a single point in time.** The most famous line is: "It was a dark and stormy night." But there are many examples of how a single point in time is the starting point. Again, think of the classic comedian set-up for a story; it's usually a single point in time.

   When you're telling a story – set the stage for your story immediately.

   "I'm at the front of the boardroom, setting up for my meeting, when the last person I would ever want to see walks in."

   "It's 7 a.m., the bus is late, and I'm waiting impatiently under the bus shelter when this man in a grey suit walks right up to me..."

---

34 Raoul Duke (Johnny Depp) in *Fear and Loathing in Las Vegas*.
35 The Narrator (Edward Norton) in *The Fight Club*.

Or, as mentioned, the traditional comedic line: *"So I'm standing there..."*

Remember the Robert McKee lesson: a story is not necessarily a narrative. To have the most impact, your story is better if it's based at one point in time.

3. **Give us a character we can connect with.**

We need to be able to picture your character and connect with them, but we don't need to know about every wrinkle or rip in their clothes.

Saying "my uncle" isn't enough. If you're telling us a story about your uncle, tell us his name and give us a few details. Is it:

"My Uncle Joe – we all have an Uncle Joe it seems, right? But my Uncle Joe is a straight up lumberjack. He's always wearing those giant heavy boots, overalls and a plaid shirt. Even to my wedding – he wore those giant work boots and a plaid shirt. He looks real tough at a glance, but one look in his eyes and you know he is one of the kindest men you'll ever meet."

Or, is it:

"My Uncle Joe – he's a Wall Street guy. Always dressed in a perfectly fitted designer suit, walking with purpose and staring people down with those piercing eyes. If I didn't know that he loves to sing karaoke on the weekends and eat chocolate chip mint ice cream while watching movies, he'd scare the heck out of me."

What does your uncle do? What does he wear? What is he known for? What do others not know that reveals his true character? Tell us a few details so we can connect to the character; and absolutely give your character a name, even if you don't want to use his real name.

Think about this line: "Way out west there was this fella ... a fella I wanna tell ya about. Fella by the name of Jeff Lebowski.[36]"

---

36 The Stranger (Sam Elliott) in *The Big Lebowski*.

What makes that work? You have a character with a name and you have some context (way out west). A couple more details and you'll be hooked.

4. **Help the audience relate on an emotional level – quickly.**

Think about the starting scene of *Scandal*. Perhaps it grabbed me because I could immediately relate to the character rushing down the street. I could feel the stress and the pressure of wanting to be on time but clearly running late.

Your story needs a person the audience can immediately relate to on an emotional level. Maybe the character is just like them. Maybe it reminds them of their father or their daughter. Or, more likely, they connect emotionally to what the character wants or fears.

Robert McKee explains a character this way:

"TRUE CHARACTER is revealed in the choices a human being makes under pressure – the greater the pressure, the deeper the revelation, the truer the choice to the character's essential nature."[37]

We need a few details so we know what that character wants and we believe there is a chance they can get it. It's not about characterization – which are details like age, sex, the type of car the character drives, where they live and what they do for a living. That can be useful, but the more important piece – the piece your audience will relate to – is their character.

The ideal is actually when you have a person whose character is different than their characterization. The movie Mr. and Mrs. Smith (Angelina Jolie and Brad Pitt) provides a great example of this. On the surface they are a boring couple, and they are bored with each other. They complete the same old household routines and think little of their spouse until suddenly it's revealed that they are both spies, and that they have been hired to kill each other. That makes for a great story.

---

37 Robert McKee, *Story: Substance, Structure, Style, and the Principles of Screenwriting* (New York: Harper Collins, 1997), 101.

Then, their true characters are revealed when they discover the truth about each other and realize that they are now being hunted by assassins from all over the world.

It can be an external or internal thing that they want ... it can be money, survival, recognition, or it can be finally getting that job, finding love, going on a grand adventure or achieving happiness.

Your character must be put under pressure to get the thing they want, so their true self is revealed.

Tell stories about what you do under pressure to show your clients what values are important to you.

5. **Put the words in the mouth of the person speaking.**

You could say: "She told me to get the hammer from the shed."

Or you could say: "Her eyes were ice cold when she looked at me and said 'Get the hammer from the shed.'"

A few descriptive words and the dialogue in the mouth of the character, and the story comes to life.

As you get comfortable telling stories, you may even make your voice deeper or add an accent to bring your character to life. You might put your hands in your pockets when you're talking from one character's perspective, and lower your voice and stiffen your stance for another's. You don't have to, but it will help bring the story to life if you do.

It takes practice but you *can* tell great stories and have more influence when you do. And you should.

Robert McKee writes that Plato, in 388 B.C. wanted to get rid of all the poets and storytellers because they were a threat to society. The argument was that writers "conceal their ideas inside the seductive emotions of art.... Every effective story sends a charged idea out to us, in effect compelling the idea into us, so that we must believe."[38]

Plato felt storytellers were dangerous and needed to be supervised. It's not that Plato didn't want any stories told; it's that he realized the awesome power of a good story. As a result, he wanted to control what stories were told. In Plato's *The Republic*, he concludes: *"Then it seems that our first business is to supervise the production of stories, and choose only those we think suitable, and reject the rest."*

Basically, Plato was saying that nannies and mothers should be allowed to tell their children only certain approved fairy tales and fables, to ensure that the young minds were shaped in just the right way.

Story has never lost its power. Influencers today still try to control the story; the media absolutely controls the stories that get told; and now you will understand and use the power of story in your business too.

Just remember, storytelling is powerful, so use your newly discovered power for good, not evil.

 KEY ACTION ITEMS:

Pause here and start outlining some of the stories you can tell. Again, you may wish to write in the book or you can download a worksheet from thenewbrandyou.com.

- What is a funny story you could tell in a business context?

---

38 Robert McKee, *Story: Substance, Structure, Style, and the Principles of Screenwriting* (New York: Harper Collins, 1997), 130.

- What is your business genesis story?

- What before and after stories do you have?

- What story would discuss a common objection to your business?

- Have you experienced a time when you had trouble making a decision; you then decided; and you were then rewarded?

Start developing these stories now. If you like to write, create an outline. If you don't, use a voice memo and start talking yourself through it.

Note how you begin the story – generally you want to start in the middle of the action. Make it interesting – include the negative so there is some real emotion and tension to the story. Refer back to the famous examples. Make a few notes on the key character that you're creating. Is there dialogue that you can use to bring the story to life? If it's a credibility story, is someone else saying how great you are?

Once you've made notes, put a time in your calendar to come back and develop these stories so you'll have them on hand for your conversations, writing and speaking.

CHAPTER 9

What to Do When Someone is Wrong

"Most people, when directly confronted with proof that they are wrong, do not change their point of view or course of action, but justify it even more tenaciously."

Carol Tavris & Elliot Aronson,
Mistakes Were Made (But Not By Me).

Sometimes you're in an industry or a role where people have a bad impression of what you do. Building a positive brand might be an uphill battle.

After years in real estate, I met all kinds of people who had preconceived notions about what I did.

Some tenants saw us as greedy.

Some people – even family and friends – saw us as slumlords.

Home sellers thought we were trying to steal their house from them.

Banks thought we were high risk.

Real estate investors aren't the only ones who face this type of challenge. Salespeople can be seen as pushy, money hungry and slimy. Cops, dentists, insurance agents, CEO's, priests … pretty much every industry and professional will have a group of people who will think negatively regarding what they do.

In building your brand, it's important to consider what some of the stereotypes or misconceptions are about what you do. You're not setting out to convince people they are wrong, but you can open their mind to a different reality.

CONVICTING THE INNOCENT

My Mom used to joke that she had a third child named "Not Me."

Growing up, "Not Me" was responsible for a lot of mischief. My brother and I didn't agree on many things, but we could almost always agree that "Not Me" did the thing that one of us was about to get into trouble for doing.

Thankfully, when I was a teenager my parents took in another kid, so there were now three of us ... making "Not Me" even more difficult to identify.

Of course, kids usually know when a mistake has been made or when an accident has happened. Kids just don't want to get in trouble or disappoint their parents.

Not much changes as adults. We still don't want to get in trouble or disappoint our loved ones, but it gets worse because we get really good at convincing *ourselves* that what we did wasn't wrong ... and wasn't a mistake.

How do you get an honest man to do dishonest things?

The book *Mistakes Were Made (But Not By Me)* covers a lot of experiments that show how, little by little, small acts of dishonesty eventually lead to the justification of big acts of dishonesty. Basically, man loses his ethical compass one step at a time.

The worst part is that most of us don't even realize we're losing our way when we start down this path. Our brains protect us from feeling bad about ourselves so we don't even see where we might be thinking really wrongly.

One study by a Yale Professor named Edwin Borchard reviewed 65 errors in criminal justice. Eight of them involved people convicted of murder where the victim actually turned up alive. Police and prosecutors refused to admit that they had done something wrong, even though they had convicted someone of murdering a person that was still alive.

I had to read that twice before it sunk in.

The victim of the person convicted of murder was found alive, and they still refused to admit that a mistake had been made. One prosecutor justified his wrong decision by saying *"Innocent people are never convicted."*

In his mind, maybe this person wasn't guilty of *that* crime, but certainly he was still guilty.

Why is this important to understand?

We *self-justify* in order to protect our ego. It's more powerful than a lie and far more dangerous because we're often not conscious that we're doing it. When we are presented with evidence that irrefutably proves we are wrong, we will still cling to the notion that what we did was not wrong.

It would be horribly uncomfortable to think you were responsible for putting an innocent man away for a crime he did not commit, so the mind quickly excuses you by allowing you to believe that person was guilty of something jail worthy.

If you're facing anyone with firm beliefs, you need to keep this in mind.

Lord Molson, a British politician, is quoted as saying: *"I will look at any additional evidence to confirm the opinion to which I have already come."*

Facts will not convince someone that they are wrong. *Telling* them they are wrong will only solidify their feeling that they are right.

So, what if someone *is* totally wrong about something? What if they look at what you do as bad because they don't really understand? What do you say?

Or what if they have a really strong opinion about something and you need to change their mind?

Clearly – you can't present facts and convince them of anything they don't already believe. If judges and prosecutors couldn't look at a living breathing human who was supposedly dead and admit that they had made a mistake, how do *you* think you're going to convince someone else to believe you over what they 'know to be true'?

Hopefully you're already thinking about a story you can tell. *Telling a story* is one of the best ways to create a new perspective.

It's a bit like the fable about the Wind and the Sun. Do you know it?

The Wind and the Sun were discussing who was the stronger force. The Wind pointed towards a farmer in a field and said to the Sun, "The one who can get that farmer to take his coat off will be deemed strongest."

The Sun nodded in agreement to the challenge as the Wind stepped forward with confidence, blowing as hard as it could. The harder the wind blew, the more the farmer zipped up his coat and held it tight to his body until the Wind had to give up.

The Sun smiled, stepped forward and shone brightly on the farmer. At first the farmer just wiped his brow. Then he unzipped his coat. But within minutes the farmer was sweating and he peeled his coat off.

Trying to convince someone with *facts* is like hammering them with the wind. They will resist and cling to their beliefs. But when you tell a story, it changes the context and suddenly they are open to a whole new idea, and their old beliefs might fall off like the coat on the farmer.

Story is one option to gently confront someone who is wrong and open their mind to a new perspective, but there are other options when it comes to giving someone a new point of view regarding the situation.

USE QUESTIONS TO CREATE A NEW PERSPECTIVE.

I used to work for a woman named Elizabeth Wesley. She ran a volunteer group with over 100 volunteers, mostly seniors. There were some nice perks for the volunteers, but the company required a pretty big time commitment from each person on a weekly basis if they wanted those perks.

My boss had her work cut out for her, handling issues amongst the volunteers while also keeping morale up so it was easy to attract new volunteers.

I remember an issue between two volunteers where she knew the man would get his back up and potentially quit if she addressed the situation head on. He was a great volunteer and took on a lot of extra responsibilities. She didn't want to lose him, but she couldn't allow him to continue to behave the way he had been behaving.

Instead of asking him not to do the very thing he was doing, she invited him for coffee and said, "Al, I need your advice. The other volunteers really respect what you say – and I have a situation I want your thoughts on." She blurred a few details but basically outlined the issue he was causing for her. She explained what her job required of her. Then she asked, "What would you do if you were me?"

Without hesitation he gave her the very solution she needed. She then gently said, "Al, I agree. I think that is a great way to handle this. So, you believe that everyone, including you, should be doing that, right?"

Approaching it from a place of *partnership*, he was willing to change his behaviour because it was his idea. From what I could tell, he didn't feel scolded or upset.

The right questions can work wonders. In Kevin Hogan's book *Invisible Influence*, he suggests using hypothetical questions like:

- Would it be possible to _____?

- How would you do it if _____?

- If <something else> was true, what would you do?

Questions need to come from a *place of curiosity and interest*, not of judgement. Be gentle in how you ask, but a well selected question can change the way someone is looking at a situation.

Questions work to help you catch *yourself* making a mistake too. Take this one, for example:

"How do you know?"

Sometimes I will tell Dave something like it's a scientific fact. Unfortunately for me, Dave's background is in market research (he has a Masters in Applied Social Psychology), and he often just looks at me with interest and says, "How do you know?"

Well Dave, I don't know. I just made it up actually. It would have been nice if you would have just let me roll with it though…. :)

It's comforting to believe we're right, even if what we believe has no foundation in fact at all.

People *might* believe what they are told, but they will *always* believe what they conclude.

This brings me back to the question…

"How do you know?"

It's a good question to ask yourself because many important decisions you make are skewed by something you believe that actually may not be based on fact.

Are you assuming your client won't pay what you're asking, or do you know?

Did you actually have that conversation with your accountant, or did you play it out in your head?

Maybe you stay in a job that is sucking the life out of you because you think it's the only way to provide for your family.

Or you might be spending a lot of money on a website because you think that is what you need to look professional.

These are beliefs with reasons, but what are the *facts*? How do you know?

How many things are you certain about today that will turn out to be mistakes?

We all hold limiting beliefs.

You have them. Your client has them.

Sometimes these beliefs are based in fact, but often we're just holding ourselves back for one reason or another. By stopping to ask yourself a question like "How do you know?" you might open doors to opportunities you would have otherwise assumed were never open to you. And a similar type of well selected question, posed as curiosity and not as a challenge, might do the same for the person you're speaking with.

CHANGE THE FRAME OF THE CONVERSATION

When we started raising a lot of money for our real estate deals, people with money seemed to have all the power in our meetings. At first, in an effort to be polite and likable, we'd often sit back and let them control the conversation, answering their questions and thanking them for taking the time to meet with us.

We felt we were being helpful and that by answering all their questions we were showcasing our expertise. We'd give them facts and figures to prove that we'd done the research and that their money was going to be in good hands. We'd handle all kinds of awkward objections like 'It doesn't seem fair that you don't have any skin in the deal' or 'This sounds a bit risky – can I just give you half the money as a test run on this deal?'

It was an awful experience for both my husband Dave and myself. Many meetings felt uncomfortable, and we sometimes felt like we were begging for money.

Most meetings ended with our potential investor saying, "Okay, well, let me think about it."

Nobody who left a conversation to 'think about it' ever invested with us. No matter how compelling our numbers were, we struggled to convince these potential investors that we had a good opportunity.

We started to turn the meetings around by focusing on finding our *ideal* investor, but it wasn't until we read the book *Pitch Anything* by Oren Klaff that we realized why we sometimes still struggled.

Klaff's book made it clear that we had to be in control of the *frame* of the meeting! Klaff describes frames as 'how you package your power, authority, strength, information and status.'

We realized that we had to take ownership of our expertise and focus on the *value* of the opportunity we were bringing to the table. We changed the frame from the investor considering whether to invest their money with us, to us deciding if *we* wanted to work with *them*.

Our meetings became fun and highly productive. We soon found ourselves with far more investors waiting for our next deal than we had deals to offer them.

We all use *frames* in conversations. Every time you meet with someone, your *frames* will be different. We were letting our potential investors' frame take control and it wasn't working.

Klaff says that in most business settings you'll find that your frame collides with a *power frame, time frame, or analyst frame*. It's your objective to choose a frame that will take control and be used during the conversation.

The frame we found to be the best fit for almost all situations we encountered in raising money was what Oren Klaff calls the *prize frame*. We became intently focused on *evaluating* our potential investors, and while they would certainly have questions for us, we were the ones who made the final decision about whether or not to work with them, not the other way around.

Frames are powerful, and a frame change just might be the way for someone to see the same situation from a totally different perspective. The
most interesting thing for us was that by taking control of the frame
right from the start of the meeting, we not only had people saying yes
on the spot; we also found ourselves facing very few of those awkward
objections like "Is it fair?" or "Can I give you just part of the money now?"

WHEN *YOU* MAKE A MISTAKE

We all make mistakes. Being an entrepreneur means you make a lot
of mistakes. If you're not making mistakes, you're not trying enough
things and your competitors are going to get the best of you!

The challenge isn't just to understand how to help someone see the
error of their ways; it's also to make sure you're seeing the error of
your ways!

> *"Because most of us are not self-correcting, and because our
> blind spots keep us from knowing that we need to be self-cor-
> recting, external procedures must be in place to correct the
> errors that human beings will inevitably make and to reduce
> the chances of future ones."*[39]

There are probably many ways to handle this challenge, but in my life,
I have two ways that I try to handle it.

The first is to encourage certain people to give me input and feedback.
I'd rather not have *everyone* criticizing my every move, but hiring a
coach, or asking select clients or close friends to tell me when I am
doing something wrong helps me to grow and improve.

You might not like it. I know I don't like it, but I also know I need to
know. I try not to get defensive; I try to accept the information and
process it so I can improve. I say 'try' because no matter how much

---

39 *Mistakes Were Made (But Not By Me)*, p. 223.

value I see in it, I still find it painful to hear there's something I am doing or saying that is not right or is not having the intended impact.

Think about it. Your friend comes to you and says, "I am going to give you some feedback." Are you excited? Do you look forward to hearing the next words out of her mouth?

I instantly feel defensive when someone offers me feedback. I haven't even heard the feedback and I can feel myself hunkering down and bracing for it. It's almost as bad as someone asking to "pick my brain." My immediate mental response is "Not a chance," and I mentally shut down to protect my gray matter from intrusion.

Besides being generally open to feedback, you need individuals around you who will just tell it to you straight. The bigger your brand or the more well known you are, the harder it can be to have people around you who will tell you when your idea stinks or when you're doing something that people don't like. Typically, people will want to please you, so they may be reluctant to tell you what they really think.

Consciously ensure that you always have at least one person who will tell you when you're not looking at the whole picture.

If you ever write a book, it's important to have a few trusted people read your book before you spend money on editors and layout design. Select people who aren't necessarily big fans of you and your work. You want people who are there to help you make a better book, not to make you feel good.

You're asking to be challenged and questioned, and you may even find out that your project, one that you may have spent months on, has some serious flaws. That's not easy. But, isn't it better to find out *before* you spend more time and more money publishing it?

At the same time, you're not seeking input from anyone and everyone.

You must be clear on who you are, what you're doing, and the brand you're trying to create, so you know when an opinion is valuable and when it will actually take you off the path you are navigating.

Your brand is you! Your brand isn't other people's idea of what you *should* be.

Consider the opinions that come at you, in order to be sure you're not missing something important; but stay true to you, your values and what you stand for.

If *everyone* likes you, then you're probably being too vanilla, and you're probably not being honest. It might feel safe to be universally liked, but you won't stand out or be interesting enough to get past that croc brain.

Look forward to the time when people criticize or disagree with what you're doing or saying. It's a sign that you're standing out and gaining notice. When that happens, have a little toast to yourself for having created your unique voice for your brand.

If you have to converse with these folks who don't agree with your opinions or your approach, you now know that *facts* won't sway them. You know that facts will only make them cling tighter to what they believe. Using questions, stories and reframing, you just might open their mind to new possibilities.

 # TIPS / KEY POINTS:

- Next time someone is wrong, ask questions from a place of curiosity to create a new perspective for them.

- When you're confronted with a challenging situation, change the frame so your perspective puts you in a stronger position.

- Celebrate what makes you special – toast the critics for letting you know that you're on the right track.

CHAPTER 10

How to Make Your Words Meaningless

It was a crisp early fall – one of those beautiful mornings where the leaves are changing to gold and orange and it's chilly but the sun is shining so it feels great to be outside.

We didn't have any early meetings or pressing issues, so my husband Dave and I grabbed the dogs and went for a stroll along the seawall in Nanaimo toward Starbucks. As we were attaching the dog leashes to the fence outside the shop, another fellow walked up with a dog. We smiled, pointed to our pups and suggested that he tie his dog up on the other side of the outdoor sitting area to keep things calm while we all went inside to enjoy a coffee.

He nodded and tied his dog to the fence at a nice distance from ours. All was well.

Inside, as we were waiting for our drinks to come up on the bar, he commented on what good dogs we had. In my head I gave thanks that they were in fact being good at that moment.

I looked out the window at his dog and said, "Your dog is beautiful." This comment gave the man his opening. He started telling us the story of how his dog had become part of the family.

It was a good story. He'd rescued his dog from a bad situation in the middle of the winter. I was smiling and nodding – encouraging him to go on. I wanted to hear more.

Then he took a step towards me.

I stiffened. He was in my space.

I was trapped. I had been leaning against the cream and milk table, which was against a wall.

He was still talking but I was no longer listening. I was trying to find a way to get more space, but there was nowhere to go.

He probably had no idea what had happened. I was totally into the story one second and running away the next.

When you are trying to engage someone in a conversation, build rapport, and perhaps influence their actions, what your body does is often even more important than the words you use.

Learning to tell great stories, taking control of the frame of the conversation, and asking great questions are all really important. The words you use matter, but they aren't the most important piece. *What your body is doing, what you look like and what your voice sounds like will all impact your message.*

You may find you struggle to gain attention or lose attention in an instant ... and it is quite likely it had nothing to do with the actual words you were saying.

That day in Starbucks, the nice man with the dog was telling a great story.

But, he never got to finish his story. The minute my coffee came up on the bar I excused myself and got out of there. I needed to get my space ... to breathe.

Let's make sure your words pack a punch – and that you keep the attention of those you work so hard to attract.

WHAT PEOPLE SEE WHEN YOU WALK IN A ROOM

After walking about 10 miles while attending a conference at the gigantic Las Vegas convention center, my feet were screaming in agony. I had been smart enough not to wear heels, but even with flat dress shoes, it hurt to walk at the end of the day.

I stopped at a little massage kiosk to get some relief in the form of a foot rub.

My masseuse was a chatty gal in her early 20's.

After I sat down, she said, *"Ms. successful business woman, would you tell me what you think of my boyfriend's business idea?"*

I said, *"What makes you think I'm a successful business woman?"*

"Well, I guess it's the way you're dressed, but it was also just how you walked in here with authority. Aren't you? You have your own business, right?"

I nodded. Then I motioned to a woman in yoga pants and a tank top rushing by. I said, *"What about her?"*

"Mom of three kids. Probably drives them to soccer and football all the time. Her best friend is getting divorced so they are here to celebrate."

I motion to a guy in jeans and a concert T-shirt. *"He works in construction. He's here to get drunk and watch sports."*

I said, *"Okay, one more. This one's going to be hard."* I motioned to a guy in khaki pants, polo shirt and sandals who was talking on the phone a few feet away from the massage booth.

She laughed and said, *"That's not that hard. He's here for a bachelor party. He probably recently graduated from University and works in banking or consulting or something. See – you can tell by the way he's standing, and the expressions on his face as he speaks, that he's kind of uptight, but those sandals say he's here to have fun, not work. He's going to let loose with his buddies tonight."*

It was our lucky day because Khaki Pants actually came in for a massage, so the other masseuse who had been laughing at our little game asked him what he was in Las Vegas for.

"My mate's bachelor party."

We didn't expect him to have an English accent. He probably wondered why we were chuckling when he told his masseuse that he'd graduated from Boston University the year before and was now working at Liberty Mutual. It was his first time in Vegas.

Based solely on non-verbal cues like body posture, facial expressions and the clothes he was wearing, it took less than 20 seconds for my masseuse to reach a lot of conclusions about him.

She was observant and pretty intuitive. Not everyone would pick up as much as she did, but it was a great example of the point I want to make here.

> *You are telling people a lot about yourself without ever saying a word.*

Within seconds, people will draw really important conclusions about you. They might be right. But, what if they are wrong? Or, what if they are right, but it's not the impression you want to make?

Your posture, expressions, mannerisms, clothes, and hairstyle tell people a lot about you, but is it the story you want them to read?

You've probably heard the stats regarding how nonverbal communication is so much more important than the actual words spoken. In certain situations, particularly where your verbal and non-verbal messages *aren't in alignment*, 55% of what you communicate will come from your body language, 38% from your voice tone, and only 7% from the actual words spoken.[40]

So what message do you want to put out there?

My brother is a carpenter who runs a crew. He laughs about people who show up at their job sites in suits to sell them things. It is easy to assume that a suit is the right thing to wear when selling, but **you**

---

40 https://www.psychologytoday.com/blog/beyond-words/201109/is-nonverbal-communication-numbers-game

have to consider the context of where you'll be having the conversations. If you're visiting a work site where hard hats, steel-toed boots, and dirt covered t-shirts are what most people are wearing, nobody is going to trust your opinion about the tools you're selling if you don't look like you have ever used one.

Be *you*. Wear what makes *you* feel like a superstar. Just be aware that if you choose to ignore situation-appropriate attire, you run the risk of people paying attention *only* to what you're wearing, and not what you're saying. You also may find yourself feeling insecure and out of place, which means you won't come across as competent and confident.

Most of us were told *'not to judge a book by its cover.'* It's a nice idea, but it's not realistic. We do it naturally. Yes, it's important to be aware of when you might be passing judgement on someone for superficial reasons, but it's not realistic to think that others won't judge *you*.

You can complain that it's not fair, or you can accept the reality and take action.

Think about the Las Vegas masseuse. What would she think about you as you walk by? Is that the message you want to send for your brand?

"The Pilot" of Seinfeld

Jerry: "Again with the sweatpants?"

George: "What? I'm comfortable."

Jerry: "You know the message you're sending out to the world with those sweatpants? You're telling the world, 'I give up. I can't compete in normal society. I'm miserable, so I might as well be comfortable.'"

WHEN YOUR BODY BETRAYS YOU – BODY LANGUAGE MISTAKES TO AVOID

When someone tells me they have been struggling to raise money or make sales in person, a quick look at what they do when they are talking about their offer can reveal the main issue they are having.

Here are three of the most common things that will send a strong message in any business setting. Check to see if you're guilty of any of them.

1. Touching Your Face or Rubbing Your Arms

Take a look around your local coffee shop. Identify the patrons who look like they are having a business meeting. See if you can tell which person is asking for something – be it a sale, cooperation, a job, or something else. The person who is asking is often scratching or rubbing something.

We rub our arms to self soothe which means we're uncomfortable. And, maybe you are actually just itchy ... but here's what you need to know:

Itching anything makes you look nervous.

Get control of your hands. You'll look and feel a lot more confident.

In Kevin Hogan's book *Invisible Influence*, he pointedly says NEVER touch your face, as it is never perceived as professional or attractive. It can also be an indicator of deception.

2. Watch the Feet

Influence is about engaging and understanding the other person's point of view.

Most of us struggle with that because we are very focused on ourselves and the message we have to communicate. By now you know that the most important person to focus on when you're influencing someone is *that person*.

Listen to them. **Your entire body – right down to your feet – needs to show them that you're engaged and really listening.**

The direction your feet point is a good indicator of where you *actually* want to be. If you're engaged in a conversation you'll usually find your feet are naturally pointing to the person you're speaking with. If you're bored, annoyed or just ready to go, your feet will naturally point to the door or an exit.

Most people know to control their facial expressions and even hand movements to reflect what they feel are appropriate responses, at least to a degree, but the feet are rarely trained. Because those two extremities are left to move at will, they can often reveal what the mind is *really* thinking

You may think that it doesn't matter because most people don't know about this, but the reality is that a **lot of cues are processed subconsciously.** The other person may not know precisely *how* they know you are (or are not!) listening to them, but they will just know.

Plus, now that you know this tip, you have another cue to check to see if you are engaging someone when you speak. The feet usually reveal what the face and mouth won't tell you.

3. What Your Posture and Position Says

I had a boss that had a swivel chair that would lean back a couple of feet. When I would bring him issues or ask him questions that made him uncomfortable, he would lean back in the chair and then cross his ankle over his knee. He was basically getting as far away from me as he could without getting up and putting up a protective barrier.

When I was discussing something that made him happy, he would lean forward on his desk or make a steeple with his hands as we chatted. These are signs of engagement and confidence.

I didn't know anything about body language at the time, but I had enough conversations with him to note the consistency in his behaviour. It was an easy pattern to spot over time.

Start paying attention to how you physically react when people ask you questions. What does your posture and position do? Then, check in with yourself to see how you felt about that question. You'll start to notice a pattern.

In the money raising workshops we ran, the most common reaction our participants had to discomfort was to pretzel up. They would cross their arms, then their legs and often sit with everything totally closed off and protected. The crossing of something was almost always in immediate response to a question that made them uncomfortable.

These are typically unconscious moves so you want to become conscious of your particular moves.

Crossing your arms or legs in answer to a question could be sending their unconscious mind signals that you want to hide the truth, or that you're uncomfortable with the question, or that you're not confident.

Lack of confidence is almost certainly NOT one of the identifiers you want associated with your brand, right?

Just like the man at Starbucks who stepped into my space, every single one of these moves can kill rapport in a second. Once rapport is gone, it's hard to get it back.

5 WAYS TO BE MORE INTERESTING

Imagine shooting the breeze in the arena locker room with your University Alumni hockey team after a game. A local jail is mentioned in a joke, and with a serious look on his face the goalie says, *"Oh no, boys – that's no joke. You don't want to go to that jail. It's pretty rough."*

Suddenly, the lively locker room goes quiet and all eyes are on the goalie.

He'd actually spent the night in that jail.

My friend Mike, who told me about this guy, said, "He really could be the poster boy for Dos Equis' most interesting man in the world." When he speaks, everyone in the locker room listens because nobody has stories like he does.

That got me thinking: What makes someone interesting?

What you say and how you say it are important, but context plays a big role.

In a locker room of company CEO's and executives, investment bankers and consultants, a story about a night spent in a local jail is unique. In a different crowd of people, where jail time is part of many people's family history, the story wouldn't get as much attention.

So, *context matters!*

What else is important?

I like to blame the listener when I am not getting the attention I think I deserve, but it's not always my husband's fault.

This is not to absolve my husband (or anyone else) of his responsibility to actually be present and participate fully in a conversation, but it does mean that there are certain things you can do or say that make you more interesting. Ultimately, you can't control other people, so the only part of the equation you can change to get better results in your conversations is *yourself.*

So, what makes you interesting? Here are five ideas:

1. Tell Great Stories

Here it is, yet again. I'm curious though – have you started a story database yet? As you've been reading this, have you opened up a Word Doc or started a notebook to start building a database of stories?

Roberto Monaco of *influenceology.com* originally gave me the idea to create a log or a database of stories that I can tell. Turn your story radar on, and note any experience or story you hear that you might be able to use in the future.

You probably don't want to go to jail to get people's attention with your next story, although if you have been to jail, I can almost guarantee that in most groups it would make for an engaging topic and people would certainly remember you. It may not, however, be the best way to build credibility (depending on why you were in jail).

But maybe you've done something else that was pretty unique. A few years ago my Dad and I did a walking tour of Tuscany in Italy. It's the only father-daughter type vacation we've ever done together, and while it was already pretty special, I wanted to do something that would make it even more memorable for my Dad.

He loves racecars, and I know Italy isn't just a country of fashion and food; it's also the home to some incredible super cars. Knowing this I looked into some options to surprise my Dad with something cool.

On our last day, we hopped into a car I had hired for the day. Dad thought we were going to another museum. He wasn't excited about seeing any more historic paintings or monuments, but he just sat back and enjoyed the car ride, content to do whatever I wanted.

It was a two hour drive to get where we were going. I figured my Dad would start to wonder why we had to go so far for a museum, but he just watched out the window taking in the countryside.

As we rolled into a little village called Maranello, he perked up as he saw a Ferrari drive by. Our driver was in on the surprise so he said, "This little village is the home to Ducati – you know the motorbike so you'll see a lot of motorbikes around here."

Dad started to ask a few questions about that as we pulled up to a building with half a dozen Ferraris out front. My Dad looked at me with surprise and a bit of confusion.

I said, "There *is* a museum here, Dad – the Ferrari Museum – but I was thinking we could go and drive Ferraris around the Italian countryside instead."

My Dad's eyes filled with tears as we jumped out of the car to go inside and get our cars!

I'd arranged for us to drive Ferraris as a gift to him, but it ended up being one of the best days of my life. When I was planning it for him, I didn't realize how much fun I would have surprising him and driving a Ferrari myself.

It's also a good story I can share.

Whatever you do in your life and business, you'll have stories to tell. There are stories in every situation. You just have to pay attention and think of the lessons or key points that can be made by way of one of your stories.

2. Be Different

You've thought about the words that you want associated with you and your brand. Now it's time to think about *what people can always count on getting when they work with you.*

- Are you always organized, on time and solution oriented?

- Are you always creative and thinking outside the box?

- Or, maybe you are highly analytical, detailed and methodical?

Now, think about what you do relative to others in your industry.

1. When people work with you, what can they expect every single time?

2. What is different about what you do compared to everyone else in your industry or field?

3. Can you *brand* yourself so that an association is always there?

From the social media world, Mari Smith always wears turquoise when she is networking and speaking. It's been over eight years since I've seen her speak and I still think of her on Twitter and Facebook when I see that color.

In the Canadian real estate world, Erwin Szeto built himself up as Mr. Hamilton by always wearing a Hamilton Tiger-Cats jersey when he networks. Despite the fact that I know many people in Hamilton who are real estate agents and investors, he is *always* the first person I think about when it comes to Hamilton real estate because he made himself different and created an association through branding. And, while he branded himself for a single city in Canada, he's become well known in real estate circles across the country! It's the opposite of what people think will happen, but the more focused you are, the more well known you can become.

ZZ Top's music isn't extraordinary (at least it isn't for me) but their beards are. When you see someone with a giant beard you just might associate that beard with their music.

3. Focus on What's Interesting To Others

The default question when you meet someone is probably, "What do you do?"

Watch closely what happens next time you're meeting new people and someone asks that question. Usually it goes like this:

> *"So – James, what do you do?"*
>
> *"Oh, I am an engineer at Engineers Ltd."*
>
> *"Oh, interesting. Have you been there long?"*
>
> *"13 years."*
>
> *"Ah – good. So I guess you like it then?"*
>
> *"Yeah – it's a good way to pay the bills. Ah … what do you do?"*

Most people don't light up and get excited when it comes to talking about what they do all day. If they *are* excited about what they do, I promise it will come out in the conversation in other ways.

Your goal is to find out what someone actually *wants* to talk about. Rarely does a question like "What do you do?" create engagement.

However, "How did you meet your friend/your wife/your business partner?" can often be a great start. Or, "What did you do that was interesting on the weekend?" or even "What brought you here?" can be a good one depending on the context. You'll probably still find out what the person does for a living, but you'll also learn a lot of other important things about them.

If they do start talking about what they do for a living, you can ask questions like:

- "How did you get into doing that?"

- "What's your favorite part of the job?" or

- "What's challenging about your job right now?"

Allow the person to showcase their expertise and you'll learn more about them.

What you really want to do is find a point of affinity or similarity **to connect on**. If you both have kids, dogs, a love of sailing, or went to the same school, you are more likely to find some great things to talk about.

Just be sure you're not dominating the conversation or coming across like an interrogator. Pay attention to their signals. If they are shifting in their seat, looking at their watch or looking around the room, there's a really good chance they aren't engaged in what you're saying. It could be that they have a lot going on at the moment, so recognize that it might not be a great time for them to get into a big conversation. But, it could also be that you just haven't found something they actually *do* want to talk about.

Just because you both have dogs, for example, doesn't mean it's a subject they will want to speak about. Maybe their dog is sick or has been a real challenge lately, and they would rather not think about at the moment.

Being interested in others and watching for signs of true engagement will make you an interesting person to talk to. Plus, when you ask good questions and watch their reactions, you'll know what stories to share because you'll have a better idea about what they are interested in.

4. **Wait For the Right Time To Tell Your Story**

It's easy to get mad at someone for not listening to you, but, as mentioned, the fault may be yours. When did you try to talk with them? Were they in the middle of something? For example, if I try to speak with Dave when the Canucks are playing, or it's game highlights time, I am actually interrupting something he was doing and I'm not going to get much attention at all. I can get mad about him not listening to me, or I can wait for a commercial or a break in the commentary.

It's not just a good idea for your marriage. In your workplace or even casual relationships, if you have something important to say, check to see if the person you're about to speak with can actually listen to you at that time.

It's not always a good time to speak.

It's also wise to know when to hold your stories for a different setting.

A social setting or a networking event is a great place to create engagement and interest in what you do. To take the relationship to the next level of discussing business proposals or even negotiations, the conversation is best moved to a more formal and appropriate setting.

Think of it in a dating context. When you meet at the social event, create interest and intrigue so when you ask for a phone number the answer is YES ... and then when you follow up to set the date, they still say yes. It's the same for business.

The right time to dive into business is rarely going to be when there are a lot of distractions like at an event of some kind. Use that time to make a connection and get them curious. Once there is interest, pause the conversation, and say "I'd love to chat about this when we can both actually focus on it. Why don't we grab coffee next week?"

There's a danger in telling your best stories at the wrong time. You could reveal just enough information that they don't feel they need to speak to you more formally, but you haven't actually told them what they really need to hear so they say YES to working with you.

Use the right material at the right time or it can be lost forever.

5. Choose Concise and Clear Language

This is 'get to the point, already!'

We, as humans, are less able to focus than ever before.

Keep your messages short and to the point as much as possible. But, in keeping them short, make them easy to picture and to be a part of.

A great movie can become boring by extending the fight scenes too long or spending too much time on any one scene. Even your best material may become boring if you go on too long. Practice your stories to hit your points and have an impact with the fewest number of words.

 Pay attention to the reaction of others when you speak. Take note of what makes them engage with you and what has them looking for the exit. Go back to the chapter on storytelling and use some of the techniques we discussed there.

Before you know it, you'll be remembered as the interesting expert, and people will be reaching out after meeting you and hearing about you.

You may wonder why the potential client never actually sets the appointment with you or why they didn't pull out their credit card when it seemed like you were a perfect fit to help them … so take a look in the mirror, ask a friend, and start paying attention to the little things you are *doing* that are making your influence attempts unsuccessful.

You might find that you're *saying* the right things but not following them with congruent *actions*.

Of course there are a lot of things we could discuss around body language, from what different eye movements can indicate, to the fascinating things a mouth does when someone is hiding something, or faking they are happy, or when they are feeling smug.

But it's complicated. Really, there are two important things to take from this chapter.

First, increase your awareness regarding the fact that you are sending a lot more messages than the ones that come out of your mouth. You can say the right things, but if your non-verbal communication doesn't line up, you're going to struggle to get the results you want. If you tell them too much too soon, or try to talk when the setting is distracting, you could be diluting the impact of your words. Everything you do, from how you walk, to what your hands do when you're speaking, to what you're wearing, is communicating to the person you're speaking with. It's important to be aware of what you're doing to improve the odds that you're sending out the right messages and creating the brand that you want.

Second, there are some distinct cues to watch for in the person you're speaking with, so you can feel confident that you're engaging them, creating a certain rapport, and making them comfortable. Watching for these signals will help you correct any mistakes you make so you can keep the conversation flowing and build that connection.

KEY ACTION ITEMS:

- When you walk into a room, what impression do you want people to have of you? Is that the impression you're currently sending with your appearance and mannerisms? If it's not, make a note about what things you will do differently.

- Start your story database.

- Put down your iPhone or tablet next time you're in a coffee shop. Scan the room and note the body language of people. Who is engaged in the conversation? Who is uncomfortable?

- Pay close attention to what movements you make when you're uncomfortable with a question or a conversation. As you note what you commonly do, you can begin to minimize these movements in future conversations. When you're having conversations where you want to have a strong impact and influence, keep your hands away from your face, point your feet to the person you're speaking with, and minimize your posture changes (sit up straight or lean in, and keep your hands in an open position or holding a pen over paper in front of you).

- Most importantly, monitor the movements of the person you're speaking with to catch when you've made them uncomfortable or you've lost their interest.

CHAPTER 11

But Do They Trust You?

"Do you want to make more money? Do you want to make big bucks? Let me hear you if you do."

Half the audience cheered enthusiastically. The rest of the people looked around with discomfort. The speaker said it again, louder and with bigger hand gestures.

He was trying to get the audience excited before he told us how we were going to make big bucks using his strategies and courses.

I was on stage next at this Investor conference and I was standing at the back of the room with the AV guys waiting to get my mic on. One of my clients walked over to me and asked, *"What do you think about him?"*

I turned the question back to my client and said, *"What do you think about him?"*

My client shrugged and whispered, *"He says the right things, but I don't trust him."*

I just smiled and nodded. It wasn't the first event where I'd shared a stage with this guy. I'd never exchanged more than pleasantries with him, but I was pretty sure my client's instincts were right. I knew I wouldn't do business with him even though I knew very little about him. But, it might make you wonder:

What if you say the right things and still don't get the results you want?

Logos and great websites are nice, but they don't make you money.

They are artificial. So are words.

You can say the right things and not get the results you want because people don't trust you. In the last chapter we covered some non-verbal communication signals that you could be sending that cause people not to trust you. When your words and movements aren't congruent, it definitely sends a signal that you're hiding something, but there's more to trust than just that.

Trust is built on little – seemingly unimportant – things, and those same little things can cause it to vanish in an instant. There can be little triggers you're setting off that cause people not to trust you – and you likely have no idea. And because you probably want to build a brand that people trust, you should pay attention and make sure people feel they can trust you.

5 WAYS THAT TRUST IS BUILT

1. Your First Impression

As I got up to leave the poker table at the Mandalay Bay Hotel in Las Vegas, an older gentleman from Los Angeles who'd been sitting beside me for a few hours said, "*Oh – the most honest person at the table is leaving, so I think I will leave too.*"

It's not saying much to call me the most honest person at a poker table, considering how much you lie when you play. Then again, I lost money that night, so perhaps I *was* too honest?

The minute someone sits down at the table, every single player forms opinions about that person, based on what they wear, how many chips they buy, how they get set up, and what they say (or, don't say) to the others at the table.

This all contributes to a rapidly formed image. In poker, you're thinking: will this person be a loose, an aggressive, or a tight player? Or, maybe they're just here to party and get free drinks? Will I make money off the new player or will I have to be careful?

The same thing happens in business.

You make a first impression with a combination of how you carry yourself, what you say, what you look like, and who you walk into a room with. The question isn't whether your first impression is good or bad; it's whether you're happy with the results you're getting. Are you establishing authority and trust amongst strangers quickly? Do people gravitate to you, or do you have to work hard to get attention? Consider carefully what impression you make, and try to adjust it if you're not making the impression you want.

2. **Do what you say you're going to do.**

If you consistently do what you say you're going to do, people will trust you.

If you say you're going to be somewhere at 3 pm, be there at 3 pm.

If you say you're going to follow up via email – do it.

If you say you'll ask your friend a question and get back to someone with the answer – make it happen.

The simplest little things can create massive trust – or erode it in an instant.[41] Little things really do matter.

We own a lot of rental property. One of the most important and consistently accurate criteria I use to pre-screen a tenant is whether the person shows up on time to view the property. If they are late and they don't call to tell me they are going to be late, I won't rent to them. After fifteen years of screening hundreds of tenants, I know this is a good representation of how seriously they take their responsibilities, including paying their rent on time. The few times I made an exception and rented to

---

41 Brene Brown gave a great talk on this idea: http://www.supersoul.tv/
supersoul-sessions/the-anatomy-of-trust/

someone who wasn't respectful of my time for the showing, we found ourselves with a challenging tenant.

It may seem like a small thing, but if you say you're going to drop something off, put something in the mail, meet someone at a certain time, or follow up on a specific day – do it. People will come to know you as someone they can rely on. Reliability is a highly desirable trait. If a person feels they can rely on you, it's likely they will trust you.

3. Relying on a Script

"I just need a script to follow."

I'm always a bit surprised when people get excited about having a script to follow in order to sell.

You only need to watch a bad movie or a lame TV show to see that even a decent script can sound awful in the hands of a terrible actor.

Words are rendered completely useless if you don't believe in your message. If the words are not part of your normal conversations, it's a double whammy. You'll feel uncomfortable and unnatural, so your body language will be totally out of alignment with what you're saying. You already know from the last chapter how important body language congruency is to being trusted and being seen as confident. A script can make this even worse if you're already nervous.

I spoke with a guy who calls himself the Sales Warlord. He's an Australian who teaches people all over the world how to close sales on the phone. He sent me a script to follow for my next sales call. It starts off: *"Excellent, you are the very person I am looking for, and I hear that you are a (man/woman) of GREAT taste and distinction."*

Those words absolutely suit his personality (and his accent!). But I laughed when I read them. Personally, I would *never* use those words in a normal conversation, so obviously if I used them in a sales call, they would sound (and feel) completely false.

Similarly, what's comfortable for *me* to say might be totally weird coming out of *your* mouth.

That's the first issue with scripts. You can use them to provide some structure to what you're saying, but relying on them word-for-word may set you up for problems.

The second issue is, if you get asked a question that isn't scripted, or if you happen to fall off the script, everything can fall apart.

Authenticity can shine through even if you use a script, but only if you are really being you and selling a message you believe in.

4. Associating with the Wrong People

Trust is highly transferable. You will trust the associates of someone you already hold in high regard. And the reverse is also true.

There is a guy in the real estate education business with whom I have done a few promotions. I like him and he's always been very friendly and supportive, but I have intentionally kept him at arms' length.

He closely associates with someone whose business practices go against everything I believe in. While he himself has never done anything that makes me distrust him, I can never fully trust someone who readily associates with a person I don't trust at all.

So just as easily as you might trust me because someone you trust endorses me; that trust can vanish if I associate with someone you *don't* trust.

Who you hang out with matters a lot. We already talked about how hanging out with the right person can make you happier, healthier, and wealthier. But also keep in mind that hanging out with a particular person can quickly affect other people's opinion of you, either positively or negatively. Beyond that, and the impact on whether others trust you, there are even more considerations that we'll touch on at the end of this chapter.

5. Belief and Commitment

Set your intention before you communicate with someone, because that will come through non-verbally in your message.

If you're not committed to your clients' happiness, enjoyment, success, results, or whatever you are offering, things will fall apart because people will sense your lack of belief or commitment.

When someone first meets you, there is one thing they will be unconsciously or consciously trying to figure out:

"Is this person for real?"

If you're covering up a lack of belief or you're not truly committed, people will sense it, and they will not buy in to what you're saying.

If you're encountering the same objection or issue over and over, it's a sign that you don't actually believe what you're saying. When I coached investors on how to raise money for their deals, the very thing they feared would keep happening. If they were afraid someone would object to the structure of the deal, that person almost always did. If they worried that an enthusiastic investor would cool off before they could bring them a deal, it happened. They would try to find the flaw in what they were saying or not doing, but it was never as simple as that. It often came back to their own personal commitment and belief.

Once they truly owned the value they were bringing to the deal, and felt confident their deal was the right fit for the person they were speaking with, those objections almost magically disappeared. The change wasn't in what they were saying; it was their own belief behind the words.

If you aren't there yet, here's what you can do to build your belief:

1. Get to know your own story. What have you experienced that makes you unique and valuable to the people you're speaking with? What is your perspective and opinion?

2. When you get comfortable with who you are, who you can help, and why you want to help, you will worry less about yourself and focus more on the person in front of you.

3. Find success stories. Depending on what you do, you may not actually *see* the results of what you do to help others. Make it a point to

follow up; meet and speak with people you've worked with so you can see the benefits of what you're offering. The more you see the value you've brought to other people's lives, the more confidence you'll have in what you offer.

4. Know more than anyone else about what you do. Understand your competitors. Identify where you are different and who is a better fit to work with you versus them. If you *aren't* different or better – what can you do to change that?

If you do that and you're still feeling insecure or unsure, maybe it's not the right business or brand for you? Consider what we covered in the first couple of chapters. Perhaps you're chasing a dream that someone else has for you, and it's not actually your own. Or maybe you got into this business or career because the money was good, not because you were deeply connected to the work.

There's no sense trying to be something you're not.

My Dad was a stockbroker when he was young. He was good at reading charts and he was making his clients quite a bit of money. His managing broker wasn't happy, though, because my Dad wasn't trading enough. The company only made money on trades – not on client profits. The broker told Dad to move the clients' money to something else after the clients made a bit of money – basically keep the accounts turning with trades. *"The clients will still make money, so what does it matter?"* his boss said to him.

It mattered to Dad because he knew he could make them a lot more money with less frequent trades that allowed them to ride the stock upswings longer. Making more frequent trades was in the company's best interest but not in the clients'.

He couldn't change how the company wanted to do business, so he quit and started his own business. If he hadn't, the trust his clients had placed in him probably wouldn't have lasted very long because they would have started to feel that something was off.

Belief and commitment to deliver are essential to communicating with influence and impact.

We want to believe that we trust for sensible reasons, but it's just not true.

We trust someone who is good looking more than someone who is less attractive. We trust someone we see on a regular basis over someone we have just met. We trust a celebrity on TV more than an acquaintance. There are no rational reasons to trust in these situations ... but it's how we're wired.

 If you aren't getting the results you want in your business, it's possible you're doing something that is causing people to walk away thinking, "There's just something about him I don't trust." Think about what kind of first impression you are making on people, and then assess your follow-through, the authenticity of your message, whom you're associating with, and your own belief in your message. It's possible one or more of these things are causing other people to wonder if they can trust you.

YOUR FRIENDS AND YOUR PERSONAL BRAND

In Chapter 2 we covered the importance of choosing who we associate with. If you surround yourself with people who are happy and confident, then you're more likely to find yourself feeling that way too. In fact, research has found that if you have a happy friend within a mile, you're 25% more likely to become happy too.[42]

Think back to the words you want people to associate with *you*. Then look at the people you spend the most time with. Would you assign those words to those people? If you have a friend that doesn't get a

---

42 Nicholas A. Christakis and James H. Fowler. *Connected: How Your Friends' Friends' Friends Affect Everything You Feel, Think, and Do*. New York: Back Bay Books, 2011.

checkmark in the 'trustworthy' box, you may want to revaluate how much time you spend with that person.

And today, it's not just about who you walk into a room with or sit beside; it's also about whom you associate with online and also what your online profiles say about you.

A few years ago I was trying to help a coaching client get a speaking gig at a major real estate event in Canada. He had been investing on the side for a few years and had just taken the leap into making it his primary business. He had some niche expertise that would have made a great talk for the event. However, when I suggested to the event director that he would be a good speaker, the director was not impressed. He said, *"His LinkedIn profile has nothing about real estate. He isn't connected with anybody important in the industry, and all his skills are IT related. How can I put him on my stage?"*

I'd made a mistake not making sure his online profile and relationships supported his expertise and the brand we'd been creating. It was a great reminder that you need to connect with the right people online as well as offline to create a consistent brand.

Your online relationships can be very public. This will impact the trust and credibility you have and what others will think of your expertise.

We'll talk a little more about creating social media profiles that match your brand in upcoming chapters. For now, consider that your offline and online connections will impact the brand you're creating, so carefully consider who and what you want to be associated with you and your business.

 KEY ACTION ITEMS:

Evaluate the level of trust strangers have in you when you first meet. If it doesn't seem to be as strong as you'd like, review:

- the first impression you make,

- whether you consistently do what you say you're going to do,

- whether your body language is congruent with your message,

- whom you associate with, and whether that is positively or negatively impacting you,

- and what your level of commitment and belief is.

Is there anything obvious you need to change? If you're not sure, ask a trusted colleague, mentor or friend to tell you what might be causing people to initially not trust you.

Review the people you are most visibly associating with online and offline. Think about the words that might be associated with them and their brand. Are you okay with having those words associated with *you*? Is there anyone in your circle who isn't trustworthy? Could that be impacting you? It doesn't mean you don't hang out with the people who aren't a good fit for your brand – it's just important to understand *what* impacts you.

CHAPTER 12

Creating a Strong Brand

I opened my inbox and my eyes went straight to the name I had been waiting to hear from – Joe Smith (not his real name).

"Finally!" I muttered as I got that jittery feeling in my stomach. You know the feeling you get when you drink too much coffee, or when you know you have to speak next in a group setting?

Joe Smith was a publisher at a major publishing house in Canada. I had been waiting for weeks to hear back from him.

For months, we'd been going back and forth working on a book proposal.

Everything had been very positive and all indicators had been that I was going to get a book deal. I was just waiting for the offer.

When I opened the email, it started off:

> *Julie & Dave,*
> *The marketing team doesn't feel you have a strong enough platform to sell books.*

The rest of the email contained a very polite rejection...explaining that we didn't have a big enough profile and that our audience was too small.

Things get a little blurry from there, but I remember going to my bedroom, sliding down the side of the bed, and sitting on the floor to cry. Not a little cute controlled cry either; I started to sob and heave.

I was shocked, disappointed, and angry. I personally knew several other authors who didn't have any sort of audience or community like we did – and they had book deals. Why had *I* been rejected?

Dave tried to console me: *"Now you can write the book you wanted to write, and you can self-publish it."*

All I could think was, 'I won't be able to sell enough books to matter.'

I did eventually self-publish. I wrote the book that I felt should be written, not the book that somebody thought was going to sell.

It was almost two years after the rejection that I finally realized the book wasn't for *me*. I had a message that could help people.

So I finally dove in and wrote it – the way I wanted to write it.

Within a week of its launch, that book, written by an author who was told she wouldn't be able to sell books, hit #1 – *overall* – on Amazon. It wasn't just #1 in a category. It was sitting there with Dan Brown, Stephen King and the *Game of Thrones* series, at the top of all the books sold on Amazon!

And there was no discounted price or gimmicks to get those results – it was selling for $22 at that time.

I am proud of those results. I also feel deeply grateful because that was not something I did alone. My husband Dave was a huge supporter every step of the way. So many people promoted the book for me, and Nick and Tom Karadza, Greg Habstritt and Philip McKernan generously supported my launch through promotions and downloads to give people during the launch week. Without them the book never would have launched with the momentum that it did.

The results were pretty amazing. But what I haven't told you yet is the enormous *obstacle* I had to overcome to publish the book. It's what kept me from writing a single word for over a year after the rejection from the publisher.

But before I tell you the big obstacle, I want to explain another concept.

You know how we've been talking extensively about *story*? There's one more piece to 'story' that I want to cover because we haven't touched on it yet.

Story is one of the most important things you can master to build a great brand. As you transition from one job to another, or from one business to another, story will be your most powerful ally for making those leaps and changes.

Do you know what I did there? Besides telling you a story about my self-publishing journey that you hopefully found interesting?

I opened and closed a loop about publishing my first book. Then I opened another loop about the biggest challenge I faced in self-publishing, but I didn't close it. Then I opened a new loop; although more of a concept than a story, it's still a new topic. The point is that I left you hanging – consciously or sub-consciously waiting to find out what the biggest challenge was.

We've talked about telling stories to gain interest, influence and connection. Now, here's an element that keeps people coming back for more and keeps their attention.

Open loops are 'elements' of a story that don't get tied up in that same moment they are introduced. Think of them as unfinished stories or story elements.

You are exposed to the use of open loops all the time; you maybe just haven't noticed.

Even simple sitcoms like *New Girl* use open loops to keep you coming back for more. One minute you'll be with Jess as she struggles with her love for a fellow teacher when she's a vice-principal; and the next minute you're watching Schmidt being bossed around by his power-hungry political girlfriend while Cece pines for him. Some stories tie up from episode to episode, but not all of them.

From scene to scene and from episode to episode, loops are left open, so you don't leave on the commercial break or stop watching the show forever.

Those are simple loops in TV. In-depth dramatic shows like *House of Cards* or *Game of Thrones* are built on open loops. A complex series like Game of Thrones probably has 20 or more open loops going at any one time. A show like Game of Thrones will even leave some loops open for an entire season. For example, for all of Season 5, we were left wondering what happened to Brandon Stark.

Any novel, great speech, comedy act or engaging conversation is full of *open loops*.

An open loop is when you start an idea, thought, or story, and instead of finishing it, you move on to something else.

In other words ... you keep the loop open.

That unfinished feeling creates unresolved emotional tension ... which in turn creates a 'cliffhanger effect.'

For me, it's why I can't read good fiction unless I have time off. I am not able to put a good book down.

The brain wants closure, so open loops keep the mind engaged and seeking that closure – In my case, keeping me up until 4 a.m. until the loops are closed.

OPEN LOOPS AND YOUR BRAND

For those willing to step into the spotlight, it's cheaper and more accessible than ever to build a high profile brand.

Because it's easier for you, it's also easier for *everyone*. You have more competition, and even worse, you're competing with something that is always at their fingertips – their phone!

If you are the slightest bit boring, you're going to lose them to that smart phone they are holding as they flip from YouTube to Instagram to Facebook to TSN to find something or someone else to entertain them.

Maybe if you're face-to-face they won't actually physically pull out their phone, but mentally they will still tune out.

Mastering open loops in your marketing, content and communication will be an effective way for you to hold their attention just a little longer. And the longer you have their attention, the better your opportunity to impact and influence ... and to be remembered!

THE THREE SKILLS YOU NEED TO CREATE A STRONG PERSONAL BRAND

A professional logo is a nice touch. A well designed website will build credibility. But the best logo and website design in the world will not help you build a brand if you aren't able to *think* through business problems, *write* marketing materials and communications, or *speak* with impact to your team, clients and vendors.

The ability to think well, write well and speak well is the foundation to creating a great brand, boosting your income and helping a lot more people. Let me explain.

THINK WELL, THINK BIG

Think big and you'll live big. You'll live big in happiness. You'll live big in accomplishment. Big in income. Big in friends. Big in respect.

David J. Schwartz, *The Magic of Thinking Big*

What happens in your head, how you speak to yourself, and the decisions you make will create your brand. Sounds a little funny, right? It's the things that are inside your brain that other people don't necessarily hear that will be the real drivers of your brand.

Imagine you're a singer. Your popularity is growing. You're not famous, but people are starting to know who you are.

You're scheduled to perform a free concert for about five hundred people in an armed forces community. You've traveled quite a distance for this concert and you're excited to have such a great audience.

A few hours before the show, a massive snowstorm rolls through. The snow piles up so fast that most people can't get out of their house, let alone drive anywhere.

Instead of five hundred people, there are ten people in the audience.

Your opening act goes on stage but puts on a half-hearted performance. They probably feel like it's a waste to expend a lot of energy playing for free for just a few people.

What do you do? It would be so easy to say, 'Forget it. Why go on? What's the point of playing for ten people?'

That's not what the performer did though. This is actually a true story and here's what happened...

He stepped on stage and said to the audience *"Well, I am disappointed that there's so few of you here, but I want to thank YOU for being here. I have a new song I want to play for you. I hope you like it."*

He proceeded to belt out *What's New Pussycat* like there were a thousand people watching. That singer was, of course, Tom Jones.

I heard that story more than five years ago when we interviewed Jim Randel, author of *Confessions of a Real Estate Entrepreneur.*

Jim was in that audience of ten.

I think about that story all the time. **It doesn't matter if there is one person or hundreds of thousands of people reading what you write or hearing what you say; it's a privilege to have an audience.**

That's a big part of thinking your way to success: it's not about YOU; it's about your audience (or your client).

Another big part of thinking well is being aware of what stories you tell *yourself*. If you always remember that it's a privilege to have an audience, and treat that audience – whether there are 10 people or 10,000 – with respect, it will always come back to you in a positive way.

PEOPLE ARE YOUR COMPETITIVE ADVANTAGE

I was at a conference in a hotel near the airport in L.A. I was tired of paying crazy high prices for average tasting hotel food, so I pulled out my phone and found a Greek place less than a mile away. As I walked towards it, I started to feel uneasy. It was dark out and the restaurant was located in a light industrial area that was poorly lit. There were bars on the windows of the buildings around it, and the only light was coming from the giant Hertz rental car lot across the road. I thought about getting an Uber and getting out of there, but I was too hungry to turn back. When I arrived at Aliki's Greek Taverna, it looked a little rough from the outside, but I decided to walk in and give it a chance.

The second I walked in, I was greeted by a super friendly guy who was probably in his 30's and seemed like he was in charge. I felt myself relax. The restaurant was busy, and as we chatted, he explained that this was his family business. He made recommendations about what I should order, and he told me about the guy in the corner and how he came in every week and ordered the same fish dish.

The food was excellent, but what made it memorable was the conversation I had with him and how comfortable he made me feel. I remember his cute daughter who he paraded around as I was leaving, and I remember how fast one of his staff came running out of the restaurant when he discovered I'd left my VISA card inside of the billfold (oops – I was definitely going to need that!). I've eaten at so many Greek restaurants, and I've even been to Greece! But this one I remember vividly because of the people.

*In this world
you're either
growing or you're
dying so get in
motion and grow.*

LOU HOLTZ

There are so many examples of where the real difference between two similar businesses is simply *the people.*

Think about your hair stylist. It's not about the products at the salon. It's about the person who does your hair – the skill, the conversation, and the service you receive. There are hundreds of realtors in your city, I bet. Who would you recommend to a friend? You probably wouldn't say "You have to work with the folks at Keller Williams," You are likely to say "You have to work with John Kemp at Keller Williams."

It's about the people.

If you're an entrepreneur and you have a small team, or no team at all, that means your success will depend entirely on how YOU perform relative to your competition.

When you realize this, you'll think differently.

When you realize that YOU are your biggest competitive advantage, you will understand that you must manage your energy, become known for your expertise, and continuously seek personal growth opportunities. An investment in training, education, or a vacation when you need a break, is an investment in building your competitive advantage.

When you do this, you'll also begin to realize how much value there is in what you do – because you've created a ton of value. This leads me to another lesson in thinking well.

YOU'RE NOT A COMMODITY

If you're a low cost service – you compete on price. **When you become *the* best at what you do, you have no competition.**

It's not just that though.

In 2009 and 2010, I had a membership program in my real estate training company.

All the online marketing gurus of that time promoted these low priced membership programs as a desired product offering because they generated recurring revenue to cover the cost of your lead generation. Then you would focus on moving these members into higher priced programs. Following that advice, I created a pretty cool membership group to help all real estate investors in their business. After a few months of promotions, I had about 150 members paying an average of $35 a month.

I didn't really believe in the upsell-focused model, but I thought that with a low price I would be able to help a lot more people.

For nearly a year I tried to make it work. It was profitable, but I was unhappy with it. Less than half of the members logged in to see the new content. A tiny percentage did the monthly action items. Those few that did try to use it seemed to complain about everything from tech troubles to not enough detail on certain topics. It seemed nobody was really satisfied and since nobody was taking action, I felt like there was no point.

I tried to create a product to help everyone and priced it to attract almost *anyone*. As a result, it attracted a lot of people who weren't a good fit for what I offered. It was a lot of work for me, didn't get great results for my clients, and wasn't very fun for me as a result.

So, against the business advice I was getting at that time, I shut it down.

I turned my focus to deeply help a small and very specific group of people within the real estate space in Canada only.

As I refined what I offered and became known as an expert in the industry, I expanded my course and increased my coaching prices. With a higher price point, I found my clients were more motivated to get results. Other people took notice of my clients' results and reached out to me for help. My workshops and training programs started to fill up.

When the programs were cheap, they attracted people who were essentially information junkies looking for a high. They weren't taking action – and without results there was nothing to create buzz and referrals.

It was an important lesson. Charging more meant working with fewer people but it meant that those I did work with, I could help in a much bigger way.

My expertise, the care that goes into how I help my clients, and the experience I bring to everything my company offers is unlike any other option in the market. It should never be priced like everything else.

I think that's the case in most businesses. If you don't treat what you do like a commodity – nobody else will either.

YOU GET WHAT YOU FOCUS ON

Have you ever tried mountain biking?

Picture this. You're riding your bike on a slightly declining single track dirt trail. You look ahead and you see this ugly looking pointy rock that takes up 70% of the trail. There's enough room to go by but the surrounding tree line makes it tight. Naturally your eyes are drawn to the rock.

The key to getting past an obstacle on your mountain bike is to turn all your attention to the path you need to follow. You have to 'pick a line' and focus on it.

The second you take your eyes off the path and look at that obstacle … guess what?

BAM! You're going to hit that rock, whack your pedal on it, bounce off of it, or worse, hit it dead on and flip yourself head over heels over the top of your handle bars. All of them hurt – a lot. Trust me.

You get what you focus on in mountain biking and in business.

If you are focused on your doubts, your fears, what people think of you, and whether you'll be criticized and judged, you'll run into those obstacles at every turn. If you focus on the value you are bringing to the table, finding the people you're perfectly suited to help, and delivering that value, you'll have to work hard, but you'll get where you want to go.

Focus on the trail ahead, not the obstacles you'll face.

It's not about pretending the challenge isn't there – it's about noticing it, finding a way around it, and staying focused on your path.

That's what gets results.

Which leads me into the final lesson for thinking your way to creating a great brand.

MAKE SUCCESS THE ONLY RESULT

Ask yourself right now: *Is what you're doing so far the best you can do? Are you giving it your all?*

Only *you* know the answer.

It is way too easy to self-justify and excuse yourself from doing the hard work that must be done.

I had a coaching call with a woman who had committed to calling ten leads for her business that month.

When we had our check-in call, she had only completed four calls. She was quick to justify why it was probably okay that she had only done four – they were high quality calls and would probably lead to at least one new client. And, she'd been working on her website so she had been getting things done.

I had to deliver the news she didn't want to hear.

"It is okay ... as long as you are okay with not reaching your goals."

And that is the bottom line.

The best thing to focus on is the next most important thing you need to do that *will* get you the results you need.

There are always hundreds of things you could do. You are your own competitive advantage. The stories you tell yourself and the tasks you focus on will all determine the strength of your brand. There are a lot of things you can do, but you must identify *the one* that you need to do next to move you closer to where you want to be.

Bottom line – remember the words of Zoe Winters: *'There is no short cut to awesome.'*

Thinking well is one of three key skills to build your brand. We're going to cover the other two next.

If you're interested in self-publishing, view my YouTube video series on writing, self-publishing and selling your book.

Check it out here: https://www. youtube.com/ user/ julieabroad

CHAPTER 13

Write Well

Yesterday my husband Dave received an unsolicited email. It said, *"Dave, thought you might be interested in this commercial deal. If you aren't, maybe you know someone who is?"* There was an email signature and a PDF of a deal somewhere in northern Alberta.

Dave forwarded it to me with a note, *"Do we know this guy?"*

We looked him up and he wasn't even a subscriber to our real estate newsletter; and since he didn't personalize the email at all, we assumed it was spam and put it in the trash bin.

At least once a week we receive an email similar to that one.

STOP SENDING EMAILS THAT GO UNANSWERED

Writing well is far more than just blogging, writing articles and creating sales copy. That's part of it, but **your ability to connect with people via the written word is critical to your success.**

People are far more likely to text, email or send you a note on Facebook than they are to call you. So ... how do you make sure you're communicating effectively via the written word?

First of all, I encourage you *not* to have important conversations via text message or email.

When I was working with real estate investors to raise money, a common issue was "people sound interested but don't get back to me."

As I dug into the problem, I discovered the deals were often presented by text message or email.

Can you imagine an easier way to miss important feedback, have miscommunications, and ultimately get ignored than via a medium where the only information you have are the words – often with weird autocorrect mistakes in them?

One of my long-time clients sent me an email saying, *"I want to discuss the renewal price of the program because I am not sure the value is there."*

I had been working hard finding opportunities for her to be featured in various media and connecting her to people who would help her with her business. When her email arrived, I was in the process of pitching her to be the featured trainer for a large national event. These were extra things I was doing to help her succeed – *not* part of the expected service she had signed up for. I felt pretty offended that she was questioning the value of my service.

Even if she really didn't see the value, she should have been careful with what she put in the email, and *I* shouldn't have responded by email (which is what I did).

Thankfully, we moved the conversation to the phone to keep the relationship in place. Sometimes, with email, there can be a miscommunication or an issue that could ruin the relationship if it's not discussed.

Use email to set up a time to talk. Use text for a quick confirmation of that meeting or a quick question. Use face-to-face or video conference calls to discuss important things like 'whether you would be a fit to invest $70,000 in this deal' or 'whether you feel the price is fair for renewal.'

And there is an art to writing in a way that gets a response. We'll cover that shortly.

BORING BLOGS

Want a cure for insomnia? Do a Google search for blogs in your industry and start reading.

There are *so many* boring blogs out there. Sure, some have good information, but often they all have the *same* information! There's no perspective or interesting stories to entice the reader.

People *do not need more information*. Everyone is drowning in information.

People need insights, context and engagement to help them digest information and enjoy what they are learning. *Entertain while you educate*, as much as you can.

When I write, I want you to feel like we're having a chat over coffee. (Do you need a refill, by the way? I could use a warm-up myself...)

Sure, there's dry material that has to get covered in almost every subject area. Try making real estate cash flow analysis or legal considerations exciting or fun ... it's a real challenge. If you need to learn SEO and other online marketing strategies – there are dry technical details that *have* to be covered. But, by throwing in stories, examples, and witty comments, there's a way to cover the material and keep your reader engaged.

For example, Guy Kawasaki has written an excellent resource book for self-publishers called *APE*. It stands for Author Publisher Entrepreneur. Despite being an incredible resource book, it's also a page-turning read. It's packed with stories, case studies and insights from his own experience and those of the clients he's worked with.

The popular books *Rich Dad Poor Dad* by Robert Kiyosaki and *The Wealthy Barber* by David Chilton are essentially fiction books that teach important lessons. They are easy to read and they have plot lines, characters and stories. You learn the material without really realizing you're learning.

When you sit down to write *anything* ... ask yourself:

What does my audience want to achieve?

The question is important regardless of whether you're writing directly to one person or broadcasting to many.

If you are a professional speaker, what does the event director want from you? They want their audience to be happy, but consider who else they are concerned about. Who pays *them*? Who evaluates *them*?

If you're a realtor, your customer is the person who is buying a home. You may assume all they care about is price ... but often that's not the most important consideration. A safe neighborhood for their family, a particular term in the deal, or a specific closing date may be *more important* than price.

If you offer nutritional counseling, clients could come to work with you for a dozen different reasons. You need to know if they are having digestive issues, or if they want to lose weight to fit into a wedding dress, or if they want to prevent an illness that plagues their family. Each client is very different, and how you communicate with them will be different based on what is most important to them.

I'll take this a step further and suggest that you also consider how they are *feeling* when they get your email or arrive at your website. Where are they likely to be when they read it? What has happened in their day so far? Are they hopeful, afraid, frustrated, tired or excited?

Then consider how you *want* them to feel.

What can you offer to move them one step closer to what they want?

You don't have to get them all the way there in one article or email, but you *do* want to give them something of value that will help them.

What is *one tip they can implement right now* to save money, make money, improve their health, have a better relationship, start their business, or whatever fits with the particular client or would-be client.

In a one-on-one email, maybe you can give them a website, introduce them to someone, or share a quick insight that gives them value.

For longer, more promotional or content-oriented emails, what is a story you have that relates to that one step they need to make?

What's holding them back?

Consider what is holding them back from getting where they want to go. What is their biggest fear?

Many people are afraid of judgment. They may worry about not having all the answers or not being experienced enough. Or they may feel overwhelmed ... their life is busy, so it's hard to make the time to do the extra things they know they should do....

Knowing these are common fears, you can share your own personal stories around these feelings in order to connect with the person you're addressing and hopefully you can help them find a solution or work through their fears.

It's a great starting point for any writing you do. In a short one-on-one email, you may not include many words (short is best!), but having this in your mind will ensure you send a meaningful message.

 Think about your ideal customer or the person you most want to connect with. How would that person complete each of the following? Take out a piece of paper and a pen and write down your answers.

Do you wish...

Do you wish people would recommend you and refer you as the expert in your market?

Are you ready...

Are you ready to step into the spotlight and be known as the expert in your area?

Do you need...

Do you need the steps to follow so you can make the change from the job you have to the business you want to have?

Are you tired of...

Are you tired of feeling like you're spinning your wheels, taking courses, reading books and still not getting your brand out there?

The more connected you are with your ideal person, the better you'll be able to fill in those blanks. As you do, you'll find yourself coming up with ideas for marketing, content, talks, products and so much more.

NOW PUT PEN TO PAPER

You don't have to write blog posts if you hate it. Personally, I think video and podcasting are a far more efficient way to connect with a wide array of audiences, but it's pretty tough to build your brand and create a business without writing *anything*, until you're in a position to hire someone to do it for you.

You're probably going to have to write emails, proposals or website content. Even if you're hiring someone to do all your writing, you need to think through what they should be covering. If you do like writing, and you're willing to work at it, creating the skill to write well can build your entire business.

Look around. People who write articles for magazines, columns for newspapers, and smart articles for their own site can build pretty incredible businesses and reputations.

Seth Godin, Tim Ferriss, David Chilton, Robert Kiyosaki and many other people first became known through their writing. They used their writing to create a *brand* and *a big business*. And that may well be your goal....

Even if you don't like writing, stick with this section. Ultimately this is about *content creation* and you're going to need ideas when you hire people, film videos, create podcasts and/or give public presentations.

Robert McKee says it bluntly:

> *The art of story transcends medium. I don't care where stories appear. I just want great stories. I don't care if I read them in a novel, see them on television, experience them in the theatre, experience them on film, in dance, in ballet, or in the opera. All I care about is story.*[43]

DITCH THAT DEGREE FOR A MINUTE

The creative writer inside of you may have been crushed if you went to university. Your inner storyteller may have been replaced with someone who could be a **sesquipedalian[44] wordsmith** – regurgitating information containing elaborate reproductions of facts to project the impression of extraordinary intelligence.

During my tenure at university, I evolved into an individual who was incredibly proficient at *using an immense quantity of words to say almost nothing.*

---

43 McKee, Robert. *Story.*
44 A long word with a lot of syllables

It often worked to get better grades, but it's a useless way of writing in the real world. If you've written a lot of reports in your career or your post secondary education is still haunting your writing, it may take some work to shake the academic style of writing, but it's worth the effort.

WHAT'S THE STORY YOU'LL TELL?

It was 2 a.m. and I was sitting in a penthouse suite at the end of the Las Vegas strip with my friend Coach Deb Cole. We had just come from an incredible red carpet awards event and after-party for the International Academy of Web Television that Deb had helped to organize.

The after-after-party for winners, nominees and the people who gave out the awards was being held at her hotel penthouse suite. There was plenty to drink, but nothing to eat and we were starving; neither one of us had eaten in nearly ten hours. We started calling pizza places – but shockingly we couldn't find a single place that would deliver to our hotel.

"Aren't we in Las Vegas? There are so many things we could order at 2 a.m. – but not pizza?" Deb was beside herself. Desperate, she actually called Zappos. They were eager to help, but they confirmed that was there was no pizza delivery available in Las Vegas after 2 a.m.!

While we were in pursuit of a pizza, her suite had filled up with people. Even if we had been able to order a pizza, we would have been lucky to even get a slice with all the people around.

Deb's friend Dirk decided to head out to find some food for us. He snuck out the back entrance (yes, the suite had more than one entrance) and came back with an elaborate feast of snacks.

It was a little strange being summoned into a bathroom by a guy I'd only just met a few days before, but when I saw the buffet of salad, sandwich, yogurt, chips and other snacks, I didn't care where we were!

Deb's gigantic bathroom actually had three different spaces in it, and Dirk had set us up on the large bathroom vanity so we could eat without having vultures hovering over our snacks. Side-by-side on cushy vanity chairs facing a large mirror, we happily dug into our food.

While we were dining in the bathroom, there were so many crazy things that happened as various inebriated people sauntered in to find an available toilet. There was one guy who was smartly dressed in a white Derby hat, suit jacket and matching dress shorts, who came in three times to look for his glasses. He was frantic as he insisted that they would be in the little toilet room on the far side of our vanity area, but he never did find them.

We didn't want to abandon our food to look for his glasses, so we just watched as he fluttered in and out. Finally he gave up and left the party. Minutes later, someone came into our dining area to use the toilet, and then came out of the toilet room holding a pair of glasses! "I found these on the floor in the corner. Do you know whose they are?" she asked us. We were laughing too hard to answer – we just nodded.

Not sure why someone would take their glasses off and put them on the floor before they go pee, but hey … it was Las Vegas. There's a reason they say 'what happens in Vegas stays in Vegas.' You've seen the movie *Hangover*, right?

After our stomachs were happily full, Deb laughed and said, "This is going to make a great story," and she started talking about how she could use the story in her business.

Even at 3 a.m., after a crazy long and busy day, she was thinking about what would make a great story for her TV interviews, talks, videos and coaching programs.

She knows the value of a great story. To steal the words of Roberto Monaco (influenceology.com), 'her story radar is on.'

Turn your story radar on!

If you haven't already made a big note on your calendar and in your notebook to start creating a story database by looking for stories in your everyday life, do it now. In fact, pause for a minute right now, and think about a couple of stories you already have stored away in your mind and some potential business lessons that could come from them.

If you subscribe to my newsletter – (if you don't, let's connect!) – you can sign up at HaveMoreInfluence.com. You'll find that pretty much every issue begins with a bit of a story. Usually the story has been carefully selected or crafted to lead to a key message that I want to leave you with. And the stories often have nothing directly to do with my business.

Here's one example from a newsletter I sent out in the summer of 2015.

> *After our in-house Crossfit competition a few weeks ago, the woman who won the competition posted a picture on Instagram. It was a black and white photo of her putting on her weight lifting shoes, and it subtly showed off her lovely hard-earned arm muscles. A relative of hers posted below it: "You need to eat. Well done. Now go eat a burger."*
>
> *She wasn't impressed.*
>
> *I know how she felt. I've had similar types of comments around my business postings. Instead of hearing 'congrats' for some of my achievements, I've sometimes heard things like "That's because you're a workaholic."*
>
> *It stings. And it can de-motivate you. But I love what Steven Pressfield says, in The War of Art, about these kinds of 'compliments':*

"The professional learns to recognize envy-driven criticism and to take it for what it is: the supreme compliment. The critic hates most that which he would have done himself if he had had the guts."

So take the comments for what they are ... nothing you need to worry about. Keep going. Create the life you want to live. When you're enjoying the fruits of your labor, doing the very thing you want to do, loving life, and someone says, "Man, you are lucky," you can just smile knowingly. Luck has little to do with it, but the people who aren't willing to get uncomfortable, stand up to criticism, and work hard will never know that.

The above example shows that every story you tell doesn't have to be movie screen worthy. But there should be a point to be made or a reason for telling it.

Okay, one more...

There I was ... sitting in my car outside the Shoppers Drug Mart store, crying.

I'm not crying cute little tears either.

I'm sobbing all my mascara off ... black rivers rushing down each cheek.

"What have I done? Why did I take this stupid job? I'm not a salesperson ... I hate asking people for things."

I was only two weeks into my summer internship at Kimberly Clark Canada and I was pretty sure I'd made a huge mistake.

In this example, I didn't give all the details in the email. You had to click a link to learn more about what happened.

And the stories don't always need to be yours. Stories you hear from others – like Jim Randel's story about the Tom Jones concert, for example – mixed in with your own stories, fables, TV stories, news items, etc. – will all work. Once your story radar is on, you'll find stories *everywhere*. Your job is to choose your stories with intention and share them in a way that connects with your audience.

Think about **who** *you're writing to*, *what* **they** *care about*, and **how** *you can connect with them*. Whether you're writing a direct email or a message for thousands, that's the best approach.

And by the way, not everyone is going to like what you have to say. Not everyone will like *you*. Your job is to focus on the people who *will* like you for *you*. Your mission is to help those people in the biggest way possible and let everyone else move on to someone they connect with.

The more you bring that unique flavor of your personality into what you write, say and do, the more you'll create a brand that you *love* and that attracts people you want to be around.

 KEY ACTION ITEMS:

- Before you write anything – from a direct email to a broadcast blog post – ask yourself:

    > What does my audience want to achieve?

    > What can I offer that will move them closer to what they want?

    > What's currently holding them back?

CHAPTER 14

When Writing Haunts You ... Bring in a Ghost

Writing for *Early to Rise*, with 500,000 readers and a team of editors, writers and copywriters was the best writing training I could ever have asked for.

The first few articles I submitted to the editor came back to me completely slaughtered. Very few of my own words survived the first cut, but I quickly learned what they were looking for and what made a fast-paced, high-value, and attention-getting article.

The editor I worked with the most, who also spent a lot of extra time teaching me how to write effectively, was Suzanne Richardson. Much of her advice is still in my head nearly nine years later.

After you've written something, set it aside for at least a day. Come back to it with the single purpose of *cutting*. Enthusiastically use the delete key. Then, go over it one more time and check it over to see if Suzanne would approve – here's what she'd be looking for:

1. **Do you get your readers attention with the first line?** If it doesn't grab attention, create intrigue, or even surprise the reader, it's not going to work. A stat that is scary or exciting or interesting, surprising thoughts, unusual situations, thought-provoking questions, unexpected actions, or just diving right into what really matters can all work to get attention.

   Your first line can make or break the article, so don't waste it.

3. **Cut all unnecessary words.** The articles for *Early to Rise* were sometimes as short as 150 words. You need to pack a punch with every word if you want to get a key point across in that short amount of space.

   Cut out all jargon.

   Use active words that get right to the point.

   Watch for spots where you use five words to say something that you can say with two or three. If a detail doesn't add to the message, chop it out.

   Here are a few examples of how we clutter up our writing with unnecessary words:

   • But the fact of the matter is – But

   • You're going to have to edit your work – You must edit your work

   • Give your post a proofread – Proofread your post (verb form)

   • She has a high level of intensity – She is intense (adjective form).

   Watch your use of the word 'very.' 'Very big' isn't as descriptive as giant or massive. 'Very quiet' should be silent or tranquil. 'Very unusual' should probably just be unusual or quirky or something else that better describes it.

3. **Can you count it?** Suzanne always wanted numbers. One time she commented: *"You say it's close, but can you tell me how many steps it is?"* It creates a great visual when you do this. For example, I could say 'I work at home," or I could say, "I have a 16-stair commute to my office." Was it really hot, or was it 110 degrees outside? Did you make more money on that deal, or did you make $280,000 more than on the last house? Numbers bring things to life. Adding numbers also gives your story credibility.

4. **Leave your reader with a great thought.** Wrap up your article with an inspiring or positive thought. This was always challenging for me, but it was often as simple as one sentence that tied back to the key message of the story and left the reader with hope, action, or inspiration. If you feel at a loss for words, you can always reach back into that file of inspirational quotes you've been collecting and leave them with someone else's words. It's like Ernest Hemmingway said: *"There is nothing to writing. All you do is sit down at a typewriter and bleed."*

This is all fine if you like writing. What if you really hate writing? Or you really aren't interested?

You don't *have* to write. Blogging and writing is easily replaced by podcasting and videos these days.

Building a brand as an expert doesn't depend on you writing. Creating a great base of video subscribers or podcast listeners will be more than enough to establish your expert status. But even millions of views or thousands of listeners will not give you the status that a published book will.

A book in print is a credibility builder second to almost nothing.

Even a degree doesn't give you the kind of credibility that a printed book will give you.

If writing a blog post intimidates you, you're probably thinking that a book is never going to happen.

But the good news is that a great ghostwriter can capture your voice, message and material and create a book for you. *Your* name goes on the cover, and it's *your* words and ideas inside the book. If you hire the right ghostwriter, it will read like *you* wrote it.

The question then becomes: how to find the right writer for your book?

To help you figure out how to hire a ghostwriter and what it might cost, I brought in the brilliant ghostwriter Zander Robertson (http://zanderrobertson.com/) to help. Zander has, at the time of writing this draft, written twenty books, is on contract to write two more, and is now coaching people who want to write their own books. He has the gift of being able to bring someone else's voice onto the page. I know some of the people he's written books for and it's *their* voice that comes through on the pages of the book.

5 TIPS FOR HIRING A GREAT GHOSTWRITER BY ZANDER ROBERTSON

"What do I do next?"

I had just handed my client his manuscript after 100 hours of hard work, but I didn't know how to answer his question. This was my first book, and neither my client nor I knew what to do. I've written more than 20 books since then and slowly uncovered the entire book creation process.

You see, most entrepreneurial type of people know what a ghostwriter is, but that's about it. This creates a big problem when they want to write a book because there is so much more to the process than just putting words on the page. For decades, the book writing and publishing industry guarded their secrets like a cheating spouse.

Consider this article your personal private investigator and follow these success tips when hiring a ghostwriter.

1) Three Questions Before Starting

1. *What is your experience with this type of book?*

    Then listen carefully to her answers. Does she have the knowledge? Will she write in the style and voice you want? A Harvard trained PhD might be highly intelligent but won't necessarily write in the conversational tone needed for a business book.

2. *Can you refer me to any of your past clients?*

> If she says yes, then follow up by calling the clients. Understand that she will probably provide her favorite (pet) clients that would never say a bad word, so be prepared to ask specific questions in order to get a true sense of how the ghostwriter works. Here are the questions I would ask: How long did your project take? Were you happy with the end result? If you could change one thing about the experience, what would it be?

3. *What is the timeline for this project?*

> For the ghostwriter to properly answer this question, you'll have to provide them with a clear picture of your project. But, once they understand the project they should be able to answer this question clearly. Never go into a relationship with a ghostwriter (or any creative) without having them commit to a clear timeline.

2) Look for a Goal-Oriented Ghostwriter

Many people believe that writing is a matter of 'inspiration.' You sit quietly and wait for inspiration. If it doesn't come, you just put aside the writing project and wait until inspiration hits.

I can't speak for fiction writers; I've never written fiction. But in the non-fiction, business- genre, a book looks a lot more like a business plan than a sketchbook.

The most important time for a business book is *before* the writing starts. Work should not commence until the goals are abundantly clear and the plan to reach the goals is set.

There are two types of goals: a) the author's goals; and b) the author's goals for the audience. Only hire a ghostwriter who can focus on both types. Run far away from a ghostwriter whose attitude seems to be, "Let's dive in and see what we find." This is a recipe for disorganization.

3) Seek Out a Price and Terms That Suit You

Andre Agassi paid his ghostwriter a million dollars to write his memoir *Open*. What did Agassi get for his million-dollar investment? He got a bestselling book that probably took his writer more than two thousand hours to complete.

Obviously, that's not your expectation, but you should still consider what level of service you want from your ghostwriter. Some book creation services simply interview the author for a few hours, transcribe the interview, and publish those transcripts as a book.

Other ghostwriters want to meet you in person, interview you for 30-50 hours or more, and dig deeper into your knowledge and story.

How much digging do you want? Do you want your ghostwriter to interview some of your colleagues and clients? More detailed work to uncover and tell the story will result in a more detailed book.

In the non-fiction, business category, for a full-length manuscript, I've heard prices as low as $5,000 and as high as $25,000. Don't expect much service for $5,000. The chances are this type of ghostwriter will simply record your interviews, transcribe your words, and tweak some of the wording; and they may not be well organized either. For $25,000, you can expect a ghostwriter that digs deep into your story, searches for your best wisdom, and researches the topic as well.

If you're writing a shorter, lead-magnet, e-book type of product, you will obviously pay a lot less. For this, you can expect a ghostwriter to charge anywhere between $0.20 and $0.40 per word.

4) Ask for a Referral

I bet if you look around, there will be at least someone in your entrepreneurial or business circle that has written a book. Their name will be on the cover, but a fairly high percentage of these people don't write their book by themselves. They hire a ghostwriter to help them. I don't know the actual figure, but I'd be willing to bet that *at least* half of the business/entrepreneurial books out there are ghostwritten.

This makes sense. Writing is a specialized skill, and for most entrepreneurial people it isn't even close to being the most important tool in their tool belt. Furthermore, writing takes a ton of time – time that you could spend making sales and delivering your product.

I don't recommend you send Richard Branson an email asking for a referral for his ghostwriter, but find someone in your own circle that has written a book and simply ask them, "Did you hire a ghostwriter to help you with your book?"

Some authors hide the fact that they hired a ghostwriter, so they might say 'no' even if they did hire one. Keep asking around and chances are you will track down a ghostwriter before long. This is probably your best bet for finding a talented and reliable ghostwriter.

Some people hire a friend who is 'good at writing' or a high school or college student. The results of these types of arrangements are mixed. I can't say it always ends up badly because that's how I got my start as a ghostwriter (a friend asked me to write his book), but you will be far more likely to have success if you hire a committed professional with a system and a history of success.

Another possibility is to hire a ghostwriter online. For example, you can explore the website *Upwork,* which is considered the premium site for online hiring. If you go to the Upwork site you can search for "ghostwriter" or "business ghostwriter." From there, you'll be able to see how many jobs they have done (in hours), what their fee is, and what each of their clients has said about them. You may not want to hire someone for the entire book project without testing them out first, so perhaps hire them to write an article or a short e-book first, to ensure you have the right person for the bigger job.

5) Don't Skimp on Editorial

The biggest weakness of most self-published books is a lack of editorial support. Remember that book readers choose books because they want *the author's best work*; otherwise they would stick to blogs. Great editors help us put our best work into the world. They aren't writers. Writers create, but editors perfect. They are people with a gift and the skill to spot errors and flaws in the material you've written.

To uncover your best work, you need two kinds of editorial support – content editing and copy-editing. The content editor helps you to craft and/or improve the big picture, and the copyeditor pores over every detail of your manuscript to discover style weaknesses, content and syntax issues, and spelling and grammar errors.

These two together can make the difference between an average book and a great book. Don't skimp.

CONCLUSION

Hiring a great ghostwriter can be one of the best decisions you ever make. Hiring the wrong ghostwriter can be one of the worst decisions you ever make.

As with most business decisions, it's 'what you don't know that you don't know' that can cause problems.

Happy writing!

Zander Robertson has ghostwritten more than 20 books for major publishing houses and self-published authors. He enables world-class entrepreneurs and visionaries to tell their stories, share powerful messages, and change the world through the written word. If you want to learn how to write your own book, or you want to find out if Zander will write it for you, visit http:// zanderrobertson. com/

KEY ACTION ITEMS

- Check your writing to make sure you grab attention with your first line, and that you have cut out unnecessary words, made your descriptions specific, and left your reader with a provocative idea or thought.

- You don't have to be the one that does the writing. If you really don't like writing or don't have time to do it, hire an expert who will do the writing for you.

If you're interested in self-publishing, I have a YouTube video series to help you.

Check it out here: *https://www. youtube.com/user/ julieabroad*

CHAPTER 15

Speaking with Authority

My first talk happened by accident.

I was at a local real estate club meeting – the second meeting I'd ever attended.

The speaker was an expert in his field, but he wasn't an investor. He made a few generalizations that were misleading for inexperienced investors. I asked a few questions to clarify his points so the new investors in the room would be clear on what they needed to know.

After the event, the organizer approached me and said, *"We're looking for a speaker for the next event. It seems like you really know what you're talking about. Want to give a talk?"*

I kind of gulped and then said "Sure."

Less than a month later I received a call from the director of events for *Canadian Real Estate Wealth Magazine* saying they were about to launch their first *Investor Forum* conference in Toronto. She said because I was a regular contributor to their magazine, their editorial staff had suggested me as a speaker.

Speaking to 15 people casually at the local club had made me nervous enough. Even though I wanted to accept the offer, the thought of flying across the country to speak in front of 400 people at an event hosted by a national magazine made me break out in a sweat. But I said yes.

I had to be in the conference room to get my microphone put on 20 minutes before I went on stage. My hands were freezing and my entire body was shaking as the AV guy worked on trying to conceal the wires of the mic. I'd never worn a mic to speak before.

As I walked on stage, my teeth were chattering. I looked out into the audience, searching for familiar faces, but the lights were so bright that most of the faces were fuzzy.

I took a deep breath and started to speak.

About 10 minutes into my talk, I said something that was supposed to be really funny.

I paused and looked around the room to make sure my story had hit the mark, but to my horror, nobody was laughing!

I made eye contact with my friend Tahani and my husband Dave, who were in the front row just to my left. They were laughing. "Well, at least they got it," I thought, and I kept going.

That is all I remember of the talk – my teeth chattering, and my story that was supposed to be funny but didn't make people laugh.

I don't remember clicking the slides forward, or doing anything else, and I don't remember walking off the stage.

People told me that the talk was great, but I wondered if they were just being nice to me because I had been so nervous.

But a few weeks later, the director of the event called and said I was the second highest rated speaker of their event. She told me they were taking this event across Canada and "would you speak at all the events?"

That was the start of giving many talks all over Canada.

Shortly after the Toronto event, I was invited to be a panelist at the *World Money Show* in Vancouver. As I was waiting in the hall for our session, I was speaking with Philip McKernan, who was the moderator of the panel. He'd been a speaker at the Toronto Forum as well, and he complimented me on my talk. When I told him how nervous I had been, he said, "*I get nervous too, but I find that if I focus on helping just one person in the room, it changes how I feel.*"

Focus on the one person you can help.

Brilliant. Simple. I am not speaking for me; I am speaking for that person in the audience that needs to hear my message that day.

I still get butterflies. I still shake before I speak. But, with that thought, those butterflies are at least focused on a purpose, not on worrying about how I will look and sound.

A SIMPLE TALK STRUCTURE FOR STARTING OUT

You could be asked to give a talk at any time. Maybe it will be for a local community group or at a bigger event for your industry.

It might scare you, but you should say yes.

Speaking is the single greatest way you can build your brand and your business while potentially impacting a lot of people at the same time.

No matter what your industry or your expertise, you have a message, a story or some tips that can make other people's lives better.

And you just might find that it's a lot of fun.

But if you're new to speaking, you may not know how to craft a good first talk.

Following is the basic structure that I use for my talks, and that I've taught to many of my coaching clients to help them with their first talks. It's simple, creates engagement, and delivers lots of value to the audience. If you have no idea how to begin, this will help.

Before I share the structure, please note that the first thing you should do before you give any talk is learn about who is in the audience and what the organizer most wants to achieve from your talk.

Make no assumptions. Ask.

When you start planning your talk, you want to be certain you have a message that will connect and add value to the folks in the room.

Questions I will try to get the answer to:

- What outcomes do the people in the audience expect to walk out with?

- What kind of knowledge and expertise do folks in the room have?

- Have you had this event before? What topics and speakers were well received? Why?

- What is the overall goal of the event?

- What is the organizer's goal? (You won't ask this necessarily, but essentially you want to figure out: What makes the organizer look good to their audience and their boss?)

You do not want to give a higher level talk to a roomful of beginners, nor do you want to use bacon analogies if the room is full of vegans or vegetarians. Learn about the people in the room, as much as you can, from the organizer. Some events list their attendees. If it's an event like a MeetUp group, or one with a Facebook Event page, you can check profiles of the folks who are attending and learn a bit more about them.

At Thrive Las Vegas in 2015, Gary Vaynerchuk was one of the speakers. He said the two-hour flight he took to get there was spent on Twitter, creeping the profiles of as many participants as he could find. Basically if you had used the hashtag for the event – #thrive15 – he was on your profile to get to know you.

It wasn't so he could call people by name; he did it to give himself a sense of who was in the audience, what type of businesses they had, and what they could use help with.

That's what you do to really connect with an audience and make sure your message hits the mark.

Your job, as a speaker, is to make the organizer look good to the audience and to their boss or team. To do that, you need to deliver what the audience wants *and* what the organizer needs and wants.

The following structure makes it simple to construct talks that engage the audience and deliver a lot of value. This isn't a keynote type of talk. This type of talk is really focused on positioning you as the expert and helping the audience solve some kind of challenge with a specific action plan or specific tips.

This type of talk is great for industry sessions and conferences where you need to deliver key takeaway and action items to the audience. I developed it from giving talks, coaching entrepreneurs who have to give their own talks, and courses and coaching from Kevin Hogan, Lisa Sasevich, and Philip McKernan, amongst others.[45]

1. Get attention with a story or a question

Resist the urge to start your talk by saying 'Thanks for having me here.' Save that for the end.

Immediately turn your attention to the folks in the audience, and with a great story, powerful question or outstanding observation, reassure them that you're not going to bore them for the next 20, 30 or 40 minutes that you're in front of them. Begin your talk by fully engaging the folks in the room. Because you've asked questions and researched their profiles, and you have a good sense of who will be in the audience, you should be able to hit on a story, a point, or a question that will get their attention quickly.

I tend to start with a story. To ground myself and the audience into the story, I usually start with a time and place. Here are a few examples of starting lines I've used:

---

45 Thanks go to Lisa Sasevich's *Speak to Sell* training; Kevin Hogan's *Professional Speakers Course;* Jeremy Donovan's *How to Deliver a TED Talk;* Robert Monaco's InfuenceOlogy, and Philip McKernan's general coaching and guidance.

"It's November 1ˢᵗ, 2008. My alarm goes off at 7 a.m., like it always does on a Monday, but today is different. I don't have a job to go to anymore."

"It was my first day of Grade 3. It wasn't anybody else's first day. Just mine."

"It was February 2000. I had just been promoted from a sales rep to an account manager. It was an hour before my first head office presentation.

There are many ways you can start a talk. Tune into the highest rated Ted Talks to get more ideas. Many of those begin with an observation, a fact, or a question.

If you get the audience's attention at the start, you'll feel like you're in it together with them. They will be on your side – supporting you to succeed in the talk. But if you start off wrong, it can be really hard to recover and connect with the audience; so work hard to get this right.

2. Position *yourself* and *your talk* for the audience

After your attention-getting start, they are listening to you and will care a lot more about what you have to share with them, so now it's time to cover what they are going to learn today.

Make it a point to tell them who this is for and why this is going to help them. Focus your attention on helping them see 'what's in it for them' to listen to you.

Sometimes I've even used a slide that says "This is for you if…" and then I give them 3 to 5 bullet points covering who is going to benefit from this information.

For example, if I were giving a talk called "Better than Blogging" to a room of new entrepreneurs or subject matter experts like realtors, real estate investors, or consultants, my slide might say:

This is for you if you:

- Are tired of your business being the best kept secret in your city

- Want to make more money

- Are ready to step into the spotlight and share your expertise

- Have a website, but nobody visits it

- Want to grow your business without spending a fortune on marketing.

That tells my audience that they are in the right place.

But not every talk needs to spell it out like that. It could be as simple as saying "This is for the entrepreneurs in the room who want to attract great clients without spending a fortune on marketing," or "This is for you if you want to write a book but you don't know where to start."

Basically, the formula is:

This is for you if you want 'x' but you don't have 'y.'

Then, you can share the key points that you're going to cover and give a little context as to why it matters to the people in the room.

The key is that you share *why* they should care as well as *what* they are going to learn. Never assume the people in the audience will know why a certain step or tip is important for them.

3. Provide 3 to 5 steps or points with examples

It does depend on the length of your talk, but giving the audience some key points, action items or steps will deliver a lot of value in a short period of time.

If you have a long or detailed process, then teach them deeply how to do one part of it. For example, if your business is building websites or running social media campaigns, it would take days to teach everything you do, but you could give them five things that work for getting 'likes' on Facebook or how to attract new friends on Instagram.

One of my clients helps people redecorate their home using things they already own to make a space they love. It's interior design in a very personal, affordable, and environmentally friendly way. Rather than teach her entire process for finding the pieces in your home that mean something, and understanding your lifestyle and designing a comfortable and beautiful space around it, she could do a talk on the '5 *Unusual Tips to Make Your Home More Beautiful on a Budget.*'

Again – the goal is to deliver massive value in a short period of time. Sure, it's always nice to leave them feeling more motivated and positive, but that will fade. Those feelings will be a lot stronger if you give them something that *actually* moves them forward – closer to where they want to be.

And, with each tip or step you cover, try to include a story, or at least an engaging example. It's much better to deliver three great tips with fun and interesting stories, than it is to deliver five tips and drown the audience in details and information.

It's impossible to teach everything that someone needs to know in a short session, but what can you give them today that will help? Focus on giving the audience something they can use. If you make it your goal at *every* talk to give the audience something of immediate use and high value, you'll find yourself getting invited back.

4. **Summarize your key message with a story.**

If you've seen some of the best speakers give talks – they have a 'signature story' that they use to open up their talk. They will often come back to this story to wrap up their talks. Or they will have another great story to wrap up with.

Those stories take years to develop, so rather than put pressure on yourself to develop a killer story right now, work towards it; and in the meantime, find a good story that ties everything up for your audience and leaves them in a positive, motivated or hopeful state of mind. You'll still be more helpful and more memorable than most of the speakers at the events you attend.

Over time, you can keep working on your stories to find the ones that really resonate for you and your audiences.

Once your final story is complete, you can then thank the organizers and the audience.

Despite what you may have heard, it's not: 'Tell them what you're going to tell them, tell them, and then tell them what you told them.' You can do that, and summarizing your key messages is a good idea, but your focus should be on creating connection with the audience and giving them massive value.

The connection comes from the stories you share.

There isn't a specific section dedicated to talking about yourself in this structure. With great stories and valuable content, you won't have to tell your audience how awesome you are; they will conclude it. Plus, if you write a great bio to include in the program and give the organizer a credibility-building introduction, the bragging is done for you! It's always better to have someone else say how great you are than to put the pressure on yourself to tell the audience.

The audience definitely does need to know some of your cool achievements and how hard you've worked to develop your expertise, but *you* don't have to tell them. You can *show* them and have other people *tell* them.

WHAT PROBLEMS ARE YOU SOLVING?

Speaking with impact is a critical skill in business, and the best communicators will rise to positions of leadership.

Understanding the foundation of what makes a great presentation or talk will also make you a better one-on-one communicator.

Whether you're delivering a talk, shooting a video, or speaking with someone face-to-face, it's important to focus on the person you're helping and why.

It's similar to what we covered in the section on writing well. What message do they need to hear?

Who are you speaking to?

- Who are they? What do they do for a living? Where do they live? Who do they live with?

- What problems are they facing? What do they know about the problems? What don't they know about them?

- What solutions do you offer?

- What tips will help them *right now*?

- Think about someone you've already helped.

  > What were the results they achieved working with you?

  > What other transformations happened in their life because of those results?

  > What would have been the cost had they not accepted your offer or followed your advice?

Think about your audience and what *their* ideal typical day might be like. How can you help them? What can you solve for them?

What do you already provide that you can package up for them?

Before you make your presentation, do the work so you know what your audience wants to achieve and how you can help. In a one-on-one conversation, ask questions so you have the information you need *before* you present a solution. If it's for a larger audience, do the research and listen to the questions and comments that come your way.

Listening to your audience will tell you what content you should be creating to include in your talks, videos and articles.

TERRIFIED OF TALKING IN PUBLIC?

You don't *have to* give talks, host podcasts or shoot videos to build your brand, but check in with yourself as to why you're avoiding it.

Sure, there are a few technical pieces to figure out, but these days that shouldn't be a problem.

A simple Google search can solve the problem of where to speak, how to shoot a video, or how to host a podcast. And all of that can be done from your smart phone!

If you are honest with yourself, it's probably fear that's stopping you from giving talks, creating videos, or writing – a fear that someone won't like you, or won't like what you have to say, or won't like your approach.

I get that! But, please remember, it's not about *you*!

When you really understand that, *everything is easier.* The longer you are holding back because you're afraid, *the longer you're leaving people stuck without your message!*

You have a way that you can make people's lives better, happier or easier. There's a gift you have that you could be giving to others.

And you probably can create a great life and a good income doing that very thing.

Of course, fear will give you all kinds of reasons to avoid stepping up and sharing your message. You might think that your idea, or your product, or your service, or whatever you offer isn't *big* enough, or that you're not experienced enough, so therefore you should wait. But *if you know you can help others,* what are you waiting for?

It really is about helping that one person.

So if you're asking yourself, 'Who am I to make a difference?' change the question and ask yourself, 'Who am I not to make a difference?'

It's not about you. It's not *for* you.

Inside each of us is a message that other people need to hear right now.

So think about who needs to hear what you have to say. **Who could be living a better life if they learned what you have to teach, heard your story, or used the product you have to offer?**

You have the power to positively impact people all around you. You can create a great life doing something that matters to you. And you don't have to feel ready to do it; you just have to start....

OKAY, SO WHAT WAS THE BIGGEST OBSTACLE TO PUBLISHING MY FIRST BOOK?

Let's close that loop from two chapters ago, shall we?

It shouldn't surprise you now that my biggest obstacle to putting out that first book was the same one that stands in my way every time I step up and try something new. I feared *judgment.*

With *More than Cashflow,* there were few people who really knew what we'd gone through; we had never openly shared it. I feared what our coaching clients would think if they knew that we had moved in with my parents because at the time we weren't making enough money to pay our mortgage. I worried about whether it would be hard to attract new investors when they read about our bad tenants and court fines. And I generally worried that people would think the book sucked.

I'm pretty sure those kinds of deep fears never go away. No amount of proof or reassurance seems to really eliminate them, so I don't try to get rid of fear anymore. Even though the book did so much better than I ever dreamed, I still feel a pang of fear when someone says, "I read your book," as I brace for a bad review or a negative comment.

It's silly for me to feel that way. In the three years since I published it, the only negative comment said to my face was when my mother-in-law commented that she'd rather I hadn't used the word 'shit' in my book (haha – now I guess I can expect that conversation to happen again).

I've realize my fear isn't going to go away, no matter how much evidence is presented to prove it wrong.

But the goal shouldn't be to defeat fear. Fear is natural, and actually important to our survival. Fear keeps us *alive*. Fear tells you that dark alley isn't safe. Fear reminds you not to text while driving. But fear also works overtime and purports to keeps you safe from things that aren't a threat to your survival – like public speaking and stepping into the spotlight.

Recognize when you're afraid. Pause, and look at *why*. Take some time to understand, and then with that understanding, reassure yourself that you're safe and carry on.

Focus on what you can do for the audience – let YOU shine through. When you're clear that you're there to help, you'll naturally adopt a more conversational style.

Jeremy Donovan talks about this in his book, *Talk Like Ted*. He says:

Most TED presenters adopt the tone of a passionate one-on-one conversationalist. To pull this off, speak in your own voice with authenticity, interest and humility. Use clear, everyday, jargon-free language packed into short complete sentences. The average TED Talk employs language at a sixth grade level. Your own enthusiastic interest should shine through with infectious curiosity, wonder and awe. To demonstrate humility, assume the role of a guide who freely shares expertise, not ego. Even the whiff of self-promotion will turn off your audience.[46]

That doesn't mean you don't practice and prepare. It doesn't mean you don't polish your message ... it just means you say what is true for you.

ASK YOUR AUDIENCE FOR HELP

Remember – your audience wants you to succeed. They don't want to sit there and be bored. They don't want you to suck ... so ask for their help.

Let them know that if they give you energy, you'll be able to give them even more. Jerry Corley, in his *Comedy Clinic*, explained that the best thing a comic can do when a joke bombs is to acknowledge it. A simple, "Well, that didn't go the way I wanted it to..." will give the audience the opportunity to laugh in release...and you'll have their support again.

Your audience wants you to engage and entertain them, so make it a team effort ... they will help you if you ask. Speaking is incredibly energizing. When you get up on a stage and give the audience your best self, and the best message you can, you'll be astounded at what a good audience will give back to you.

You'll never know the feeling if you don't try it though....

---

46 Donovan, Jeremy, *How to Deliver a TED Talk – Secrets of the World's Most Inspiring Presentations*, 2012, p. 72.

KEY ACTION ITEMS:

- Focus on the one person you can help – in conversations, videos, podcasts and talks. It's not about *you*.

- Create connection and build your credibility with the stories you share.

- Have a great bio that can be read or shared before you speak so you have *someone else* tell an audience how great you are.

- Know who you are speaking to: who are they, what are the problems you can help them with, what tips will help them right now, and how can you demonstrate how you help?

CHAPTER 16

Your Website as Your Brand's Home Base

"If you build it, he will come."

Words made famous by the 1989 movie Field of Dreams starring Kevin Costner.

Maybe, when you're talking about a beloved sport like baseball, there is some truth to that statement. Maybe.

When you're talking about a website, it's just one amongst **892,743,625**[47] **other websites**. When you know there are nearly a billion other websites out there, can you really believe that if you build it, people will visit it?

That's not to diminish the importance or the value of your website. The time we live in is special. We can make a great living from the comfort of our own home – working with people anywhere in the world. We can shoot videos and upload them with little more than our smart phone and an internet connection, and reach 1,000,000 people in hours.

We really can live and work anywhere we want to now. My business goes anywhere I do. That's a blessing and sometimes a curse, but it's mostly a gift I never stop being grateful for.

There's no worry about moving my store or finding new clients when I move; it all moves seamlessly with me.

---

47 http://news.netcraft.com/archives/category/web-server-survey/

But even for an online business like mine, a website is not everything. Your website is not your brand; you are. Relying solely on a website to be your brand will not work.

A website is not a magic bullet.

You have to actively drive traffic to your website, network with people in your industry, and get yourself in front of other people's audiences on a regular basis.

There are exceptions to every rule, but most people are going to have to work really hard to stand out amongst the billion other websites out there. And, despite your best efforts, you may find that it's a real struggle to get more than a few hundred visitors to your website each month.

Are you okay with that?

"Gee Julie. Thanks for the pep talk!" – right?

You have to know what you're in for. And if you prepare for a massive amount of work and then it happens to be easier than you thought, that's great news.

Most people get a few steps into building their online brand and find out that it's really hard work. Then they look around and think, "There has to be an easier way." And off they go to a new course or even a different job.

Maybe it will be easier for you, but every achievement I've had in business has come on the back of some seriously hard work, setbacks and tough choices. Even knowing that, it's still often more difficult than I expected.

But that's okay. It just means there will be even fewer people for me to compete with, because I know many people will turn back and give up, rather than push forward. I will push forward; will you?

Success is committing to do whatever it takes, at the same time knowing that you may not get where you want to go. But you might, and that's exciting.

Will my husband Dave ever get a starring role in a cool TV show or an awesome big production movie project?

Will anybody read this book? Will anybody be happy enough about it to write a 5-star Amazon review and tell others to read it?

Will lots of people find your website, join your community, and hire you to do the thing you specialize in?

I hope so; I really do. But I don't know. And you don't know.

The only thing you do know is that if you don't try – if you don't commit to it and give it an all-out effort – you'll never know.

The magic bullet you're looking for is within you – it's your commitment to creating the life you want to live and helping others along the way. If you're only interested, and not committed, you won't have enough juice to keep going for the squeeze.

DONE IS MORE IMPORTANT THAN GOOD

In an interview with Marie Forleo, Elizabeth Gilbert, author of *Eat, Pray, Love*, talks about how many 'good books' are only partially written, and she states that *"Done is more important than good."*

She said that as she was writing her first book, she realized it was total garbage ... but she finished it anyway. Her contract with herself was to finish what she had started.

If you're launching your first website, get it done. I can't imagine how many partially finished websites are unpublished in the world. Get it 'good enough' and hit 'publish.'

You can change it later. Just remember that *done* is better than *good*.

WHAT YOUR WEBSITE NEEDS TO HAVE

Your website isn't everything, but it is important.

When someone lands on your website, it should be clear:

- Who you are,
- How you help (and who you help),
- And, that you will add value.

The words you want associated with your *brand* should be the same ones that are associated with your *website*.

As we discussed in Chapter 5, you want your website to show up on Page 1 when someone searches your name. Your website needs to be *optimized* so that happens.

Once you have your name controlled as best you can on Google, you will want to move on to *keywords*. If you're focused on a local market, you definitely want to be the person that is found in the top spots for 'your service + your city' searches.

Identify the common keywords that you want to show up in search results for, and then focus on creating some great content on your website around those words.

There are plenty of other sources of information out there that will help you with your ranking on Google. I've found that the Wordpress plugin *SEO Yoast* is brilliant and does a lot of the hard SEO work for you. Install it, make sure you get a green light for all your posts and pages, and you're good to go.

More importantly, take note that Google is not going to be your only source of traffic. You need to work on driving traffic in many ways. It can be a lot of work to attract people one at a time, so one of the best uses of time is to get in front of someone else's audience. Write an article for big blogs or news sites in your niche (and get a link back to your website); speak at local and industry specific events; and partner with people who have complementary services so they can promote what you offer to their audience (and vice versa).

A Google lead is pretty cold; you have to work hard to develop a relationship. But when someone else puts you in front of their audience, the trust those folks have in that person (or that company) gets transferred to you.

However, no matter *how* a visitor gets to your website, when someone comes to your website, **your goal is to build a relationship with that person.**

To me, the goal of everything you do online is *to send people back to your website* where you begin to build a relationship with them.

You can direct people to subscribe to your YouTube Channel, 'like' your Facebook page, or Tweet with you on Twitter, but you don't *own* any of those spaces. You're a tenant that doesn't pay rent. One day the landlord may decide to throw your freeloading butt out or raise the rent.

You may not like it, but you are *using* the space and you have to play by their rules. One of the rules seems to be that the rules are subject to change at any time.

So unless you want to be totally at the mercy of your landlord, you should build a community that you control. To do that, you'll want people to be opting in to a list that *you* own.

Note that to encourage someone to give you their email address or phone number, you typically need to give them something so valuable they would otherwise have to pay for it.

Jon Morrow of BoostBlogTraffic.com calls this a 'Lead Magnet.'

Great lead magnets include checklists, blueprints, video training, reports, etc. Again, the key is that these things are so valuable someone would pay for them. And a great lead magnet should provide *immediate* value.

I referenced **Jon Morrow** here because I think he really dominates in this area. I've sent hundreds of people to his website to download his free magnet 'Headline Hacks' because it's so valuable in creating great article titles. In fact, most of the blog posts on his website are so valuable I would pay to read them.

And, that's what you want. Content that is so valuable someone would pay to access it.

If you offer garbage, you might get someone to sign up, but once they see what you've given them, they will unsubscribe and may even flag your email as SPAM. They certainly won't pay you for any services or stick around to have a relationship with you.

You're better off to give them a beautifully designed one-page checklist or flow chart that is super useful rather than a 20-page report that is mediocre.

Think of this like a date. If you asked someone out with the promise of a great first date, and then took them to a cheap little restaurant, are you going to get a second date?

Make a *fabulous* first impression. If you aren't ready to give them a five-star experience, don't promise that. Promise them a great cup of coffee and deliver on it! And give them a biscotti to go with it.

You met and hopefully exceeded their expectations.

Now you have a second date.

THREE IMPORTANT WEBSITE TIPS:

Is It Clear What Your Visitor Should Do First?

When someone arrives at your website, you want it to be clear what your site is about (who it's for and what you do) and what you want them to do. You may have a variety of website objectives, from having them sign up for your newsletter to selling them something. But what is the *first* thing you want them to do?

For many businesses, this will be to sign up so you can connect with them later. But, you may want them to call you. Make that clear to your website visitors.

There are a lot of potential things on your website for a visitor to click on – from content to links about you and your products or services – and you want to make sure that your visitor knows what they should do first. *Make it easy and obvious.*

Who Is Your Website For?

In creating a website that is about building your brand and establishing you as the expert, it's easy to fall into the trap of thinking that this website should be all about *you*. But it shouldn't be.

Read your copy ... *is it about you or about your client?*

Even your *About Me* page is really for your client. What do they need to know about you? Why should they care that you have certain expertise or certain experience? What does that mean for them? If it's not obvious, explain!

 Ask colleagues, friends or a trusted mentor to read your 'About Me' page. Ask them if they felt it was helpful to them, or if it just felt like you were bragging about yourself. Your goal is to have your About Me page communicate important information about you that your client needs to know and to deliver a few points of *connection*. Mix business with your personality to get a great About Me page.

Your brand is *you*, but you're not in business without *them*. Show them you know who they are and explain how you'll make their life better, easier and/or more fun.

Show Your Face!

In an attempt to look like a large company, a lot of entrepreneurs and professionals use the word 'we' and try to imply that they have a big organization. As a result, they skip important details like their picture or their bio. Or they make things really generic so it could actually be almost anybody's website.

Real estate investors often fall into this trap, thinking they need to look like a big company to raise capital for their deals. They create a corporate type website complete with mission statements, corporate objectives and investment portfolios, as if they have millions and millions of investment capital in their pool. To reinforce that idea, the website lists every person on their team including their accountant, lawyer, mortgage broker, real estate agent, general contractor and cleaning lady.

If you aren't a big company, why pretend?

Your ideal client isn't interested in working with a giant corporation; if they were, they wouldn't be your ideal client.

You don't need to be something you're not.

Your ideal client wants to know who YOU are, why you are the right person to help them, and what you can do for them.

Your website is your home base. Make it something you're proud of, but know that you can always improve it, add to it, and make it even better as you go. In the meantime, *get it out there.*

A QUICK NOTE ABOUT YOUR URL

A smart URL and brand name can make your business. 1-800-Got-Junk wouldn't be the company it is today without that number and website locked down. And it wasn't an easy get either. It took a massive amount of persistence to get that number across every state and every province.

That was smart corporate branding.

If you're not sure where to start with your URL, why not start with your name? You want to own your name online anyway because you want to control your online space. If you change your mind and want a different URL in the future, it's not that complicated to move it and redirect links.

HaveMoreInfluence.com started as JulieBroad.com. I didn't know what to call it when I started so I began with my name. Some of my videos even reference JulieBroad.com. Eventually, I switched it to Have More Influence so that it's more connected to what I help others do. Now, JulieBroad.com just redirects to HaveMoreInfluence.com.

Whatever you decide, may I suggest you avoid a mistake that I made? My first online business was built on revnyou.com. It's pronounced 'revenue.' When my husband and I started our newsletter in 2006, we loved that the name could do double duty – making revenue from real estate and motivationally putting the 'rev in you.'

We always had to spell the URL out. Even then, people weren't sure they had it right because it looked weird. Even our clients were unsure how to pronounce it, and the URL didn't have any keywords to tell Google (or anyone else) what the website was about. We built it into a decent niche brand in Canada, but it was far from being an ideal URL.

Create a website URL that uses a common ending like .com, .org, .net (or .ca for Canadians) and that is:

- Simple to say

- Easy to spell

- Short

- Not too similar to something else in your industry.

Your URL should be the brand you're going to promote but it does not have to be the same name as your business. My actual business name is Rev N You Training Inc. That's not what I promote though. I promote my own name and my website: HaveMoreInfluence.com.

NO WEBSITE RIGHT NOW? KEEP IT SIMPLE

As you build your brand, people *will* search for you online. You can do business without a website, but you will be missing out on a lot of leads without one. It would be ideal if you at least have a basic site so there's something for people to find when they type your name into Google.

If you don't have a website right now, you may feel overwhelmed at the thought of having to set one up. My best advice is to use WordPress. Buy a nice theme that gives you a look and feel you like (I like WooThemes Canvas but there are plenty of great options out there). Make sure it's a 'responsive' theme, which means it's mobile friendly and will work well on a variety of platforms. Then hire someone to design some graphics for you. You can hire someone through Fiverr.com, 99Designs.com or UpWork.com. Check the past customer comments and read the terms carefully so you know how many revisions you can ask for, what you need to provide, and what format your graphics will be delivered in. You can also use a site like Canva.com to create your own banners if you have a good eye for color and design.

The key content pages you need to focus on right now include (in order of priority):

1. Home Page – clearly showing the value you are offering to your audience, and ideally connecting with them right away. Your future goal should be to provide a few pieces of high value content to get

visitors to your site immediately. This also showcases your expertise. For most businesses, the most important thing for your home page is the invitation to connect with you. This might be through signing up for your podcast, newsletter, video updates or whatever you are going to do. Possibly, it's to book a call with you or meet you in person somewhere. This is probably the most important piece. Even if you aren't ready to launch a full website, you should have something on your URL that allows you to build your community and connect to the leads that are coming your way.

2. About Me Page – again, focus on what your ideal client needs to know about you. You absolutely need to include your picture on this page, and a great write-up about who you are and how you can help them. If you've been in the media or won any awards, you can include that here too.

3. Services and Products – even if you have nothing to offer right now, let them know what you are going to have available to help them in the future.

You may not have any content ready yet, and that's okay. Start here, and then build a plan to create content in the future. We'll talk about content in the next chapter.

DO YOU NEED A LOGO?

Twitter bought their logo off iStockPhoto for $15. CocoCola's logo was originally suggested by their bookkeeper. Google's logo was created by one of the cofounders using a free program.[48]

You can spend $1,000 or more getting a custom-designed logo, but that's not a good use of your time or funds right now. If you do decide to get a logo, you don't have to spend a ton of money. And if you do have one made, remember the words you want associated with your brand. But you don't *need* a logo. Not having a logo should not hold

---

48 http://www.entrepreneur.com/article/232401

you back from doing the thing you want to do. Neither should the right URL or business name.

Start doing what you want to do ... see if people want to pay you for it, and see if you like it.

It's like in real estate. People would come to me for coaching to become a full time real estate investor, but they'd never bought even one investment property. How can you plan your entire life around something when you don't really know if you're going to like it?

Try coaching someone for free or offering your service one-on-one to someone before you worry about whether you look like a professional business. Make sure you're adding value and having fun doing it.

 Where you *should* spend a few bucks and put in some effort is getting a great head shot!

You can usually hire a professional photographer for less than $200. *Do* hire a professional; it's worth it.

This one image can change the trajectory of your career.

Don't believe me? Ask any actor how important a great headshot is.

Your website makes a great home base for your brand and your business. Owning your name and showing up in search results is only going to grow in importance. It *is* something to pay attention to and put some time into.

We're going to get into social media next, but for now, the basic goals for your website are: it should reflect the brand you want to create, and it should clearly connect with your ideal client and begin building a relationship.

It's not the magic bullet to building your brand and making money, but it can be a great tool in your branding tool box if you take the time to think through the important elements and focus on adding value for the people you most want to connect with.

KEY ACTION ITEMS:

- If you haven't already, buy your name as a URL (I use Name Cheap but there are plenty of places to buy website names).

- Optimize your website to show up on Google for your name and a few key words that are important to your business.

- Make sure your website is clear about who you are, who it's for, and what you want visitors to do first.

- Create a great lead magnet – something so good that people would pay money for it. Then focus your traffic driving efforts on getting in front of other people's audiences.

- Get a great professional head shot.

CHAPTER 17

Marketing To the Future

Imagine it's Sunday afternoon. You've spent the morning doing work around the house, and with that satisfied feeling that comes with a completed checklist, you're ready to relax. You think, "I'd love to just chill and watch a movie."

No problem, right? You flop down in front of your TV, open up the Netflix app, see what is recommended, read a couple of reviews, and hit 'play.'

Now imagine it's 2008. You probably feel like you have to comb your hair and put on something other than your sweat pants so you can go out to the local rental store. You get changed, walk the 10 minutes to the store and start wandering the aisles.

You see a couple of movies that look okay, but you aren't sure. You ask the guy behind the counter. He tries to be helpful, but he hasn't seen either of the movies you're asking about. Someone in line says the one movie was pretty good if you like blood and guts....

Feeling unsure, you decide to rent both movies. Eight dollars and nearly an hour after you decided to watch a movie, you sit on the sofa and begin to relax.

How we consume content is dramatically different today than it was just 10 years ago ... even five years ago.

We stream TV shows without any advertising at all. We get our newspapers, magazines and books online where we can avoid a lot of ads.

Marketing isn't dead, but it's evolving.

The good news is that it's easier than ever to reach your audience. For a very small cost, you can do things that weren't even an option to a small entrepreneur or individual in the past.

You want to be on TV? Create a great YouTube channel filled with fun and interesting videos. You can become a household name in your niche without ever landing a TV deal. You may even strike it rich like some YouTubers have, creating content viewed by millions and getting paid for product endorsements. You want a radio show of your own? Launch a podcast and put it on iTunes. With Apple CarPlay in many new cars, your potential audience is expanding quickly.

You want to be a published author? No problem! No book deal needed anymore. The development of e-readers means that anyone can be a published author, and you don't even have to take on the expense of printing your book. When someone wants to read your book, they can get it in seconds by downloading it to their tablet or e-reader device. No going to a store or waiting for it to arrive in the mail.

With the growth in channels and networks, there will be less money for production companies to make on distributing their show. Our favorite shows will make more money working in product placement and actor product usage. When our favorite character is eating a sub (*Chuck*) or using an iPad (*Modern Family*), it often makes us want to do the same thing, even if we don't consciously think about it.

Like it or not, marketing has evolved from in-your-face ads that you can ignore to being embedded in high-quality content you want to consume.

Big companies have had to change what they do to get attention, and you will have to as well. The good news is that your ideal clients are hanging out somewhere online already ... you just have to find them.

Find where your ideal contacts are hanging out. What platforms are they using? What are they watching and reading? How can you create something of value that they are already hungry for, and put it on a platform that they are already hanging out on?

If you find that your ideal client is on YouTube, it's not enough to create a YouTube video. What are you doing to make your videos stand out from the millions of other videos being posted?

Your initial goal is to build a relationship.

Give massive value before you ask for anything.

If you let an intense focus on *sales* – and what is in it for you – drive what you do, you'll probably struggle with marketing your brand.

Obviously you're in business to make a profit, but the more you focus on delivering massive value to your ideal customer, the less you have to worry about making money. It just happens.

Of course, there's more to it than that, but when you sit down to consider how you'll get your message out, remember it's about your *customers* and what you can do for them.

HOW OFTEN TO CREATE CONTENT

Great content is often the foundation of an expert's brand. It also gives you something valuable to share on social media.

Well-crafted content showcases your expertise and can grow your network if you create content that people search for, share and save. Depending on your business model, you may not need to post regular content to your website. Many professional speakers, for example, just need a website that functions as an online speaker's kit. They need a brilliant demo reel, some photos showcasing them in action, and then they occasionally add articles or videos from their talks or media appearances.

You may hear that you need to post twice a week, or email every day, or publish a newsletter weekly, but it depends on your business model and what you're driven to do. Regular content creation helps you in the eyes of Google and will keep you more top of mind, but it does depend on what you want to accomplish and who you want to connect with.

Peter Shankman, Angel investor, entrepreneur and author, publishes new content monthly. That's it. He even says that on his website when you sign up for his newsletter.

Tonya Reiman, who is considered America's body language expert by many news and media outlets, doesn't post regular content to her website at all. She was on the O'Reilly Factor on Fox for years and is a regular on many American media outlets to discuss political debates or celebrity scandals. She doesn't post regular content to her website, but when there is something interesting happening, you should see the *amazing discussion and debate* on her personal Facebook page! She connects with her fans and friends through Facebook and it works for her.

Other people commit to hitting your inbox on a regular basis. 'Coffee with Kevin Hogan' hits your inbox almost every Sunday. Marie Forleo's video tip hits your inbox almost every Tuesday. My 'Broad Thoughts' newsletter will arrive in your inbox about 40 Mondays a year.

There isn't one way to succeed. It's up to you to figure out what works for you and your audience.

Stay on top of your site so you don't have errors that go unnoticed for months at a time (and if you ever notice an error on my site, please let me know!) Showcase your expertise in a way that you enjoy and that your audience engages with; and most importantly, have fun with it. If it's not fun or enjoyable, find a new approach that is!

To help you manage the ideas you have right now and create a plan for the content you put out there, you may want to create a *content calendar* for yourself. It doesn't have to be complicated, but it will help you think through the material you want to cover, when you want to post it, and where it will be promoted.

If you have courses, products or events coming up, you may want to schedule content that will help promote them. For example, I have an event to help you build your business through branding. Around that event I will put out more videos with tips to help you around building your brand or having conversations that sell. The idea is to give a tip that will help and to let the viewer or reader know that if they want the entire process, there's an event where they can get it all.

The big thing is to consider, in advance, what topics you want to cover. It is always easier to know in advance what you're going to write about or talk about than it is to force yourself to sit in front of the computer or camera and come up with in on the spot.

 If you want an example of a content calendar I use, you can download it here: thenewbrandyou.com

LET'S BE SOCIAL WITH SOCIAL MEDIA

You can waste a lot of time on social media and not get any results at all.

A lot of people get sucked into the void of cute kitten videos, selfie pictures, and comparing themselves to others. But if you want to build your brand, focus instead on adding value and entertaining those you connect with.

If you genuinely do not like social media, don't sweat it. In fact, if you don't like social media at all, make that part of your brand! Be the guy or gal that refuses to join a single platform and you'll deeply connect with the other people who feel the same way. Your challenge is that you will then have to find other ways to connect with them because you won't be able to use these online gathering places to find them.

If you get in front of enough people and always add value, nobody will care that you never post, tweet or pin anything.

Try not to sweat it. Instead, focus on finding a platform that you like, consistently share good content, and build a following.

There's a lot more out there than Facebook and Twitter.

For example, the website Quora is a fun and useful place to spend time and showcase your expertise. It's all about questions and the best answers. That might be the perfect place for you to showcase your expertise, and you'll never have to look at pictures of people's meals or their selfies. Just remember to investigate whether your ideal client that you want to connect with is also hanging out there.

Be your fabulous self in a space that suits you, your personality, and the brand you're trying to create. Post what matters to you and what matters to the people you want to connect with.

Keep it simple so you can stay sane.

Put your credit card away. You don't need a social media guru or a team of Tweeters, and you shouldn't waste money buying likes or followers. In many cases, if you're paying for followers, views, and subscribers, you are violating the terms of the agreement you have with that platform. YouTube, for example, is watching for people who buy subscribers; it's against their terms of service, and they can disable your account and even delete it.

So it's just not worth it, even though it might be *tempting* when you have to ask all your friends and family to follow, like and subscribe to your stuff so you have a few warm bodies on your profile.

WHY SOCIAL MEDIA CAN BE GREAT

It's not mandatory for a strong brand; however, being active on one additional platform outside of your website *can* be really beneficial if you are able to bring your personality into it. It's a simple way to go where the people are already hanging out, versus trying to attract people to hang out at your website when it's new. And, as we discussed before, it can also help you bury unwanted links and images if you have those showing up in Google Searches. Here are some other benefits to using one social media platform to help build your online presence and your personal brand:

- **Creating connections**. I actually started a business called Diva Money Club with three ladies I met online. As we got to know each other, we found we all wanted to help women create financial independence. We joined together, had a ton of fun, and for a year we ran a business that did just that. That opportunity arose because of our blogs and Facebook posts.

  Social media is a great way to connect with others when you're at large conferences and events. You can check the event hashtag (I mentioned how Gary Vaynerchuk used the #thrive15 hashtag to research attendees before he spoke at Thrive in Las Vegas). By searching through the other people using that hashtag, you might find some great people you can hang out with and build relationships with while you're at the same event. It also allows you to find people with similar interests.

  The big thing with online connections is that *to really create a relationship you do have to take them offline by speaking on the phone or meeting face to face.*

- **Sending traffic to your website.** You can post your content so others can easily share it … reaching the friends of your friends, and so on.

- **Providing a place where your audience can engage with you**, and you can learn about them. Social media provides you with a way for potential clients to comfortably reach out to you. This is important because people will do business with people they feel they know, like and trust. Plus, digesting what people say about your posts, and observing what posts get comments and what questions get asked in response, will teach you a lot about the people you're connecting with so you can help them in an even bigger way.

- **Data.** Understanding *who* you are connecting with and what content is working is some pretty cool information that you can use to refine what you do in the future. Google Analytics gives you some great data, but diving into the information you can collect from Facebook, Twitter, and YouTube, you can learn even more about your audience. On YouTube, for example, you can see at what point people lose interest in your video. In all of the platforms, you can see who connects with you (subscribes, likes, follows, etc.), and check out their profiles to learn more about them including information like TV shows they watch, books they read, and other pages, groups or companies they like. You may begin to spot a trend amongst your audience that will help you deepen your connection and create content that is even more relevant to them. Of course, they may have protected their information, but many people will have some information accessible. It's an opportunity for you to better connect with the people in your audience by understanding more of their personal information.

- **A way to promote for others.** This is a value add you can offer to the people who trust you enough to share your work with their audience. When you *do* get invited to speak or guest post, or you get interviewed in the media, having social media to share it on is a big benefit to everyone. They will appreciate the social media activity, and your audience will appreciate the content.

- **Paid advertising.** It's also a great place to run some very targeted ads. Smartly crafted ads can connect to those who are looking to solve a problem or learn more about something. Because you can target really specific groups of people, the right message can be highly successful.

Again, you don't have to use social media, but it might be worth finding one platform you like just to take advantage of the benefits listed above.

5 SIMPLE SOCIAL MEDIA TIPS FOR PERSONAL BRANDING

1. Your profile picture should be a great close-up shot of you. Your kids are cute, but unless they are to be the face of your brand, *you* need to be highly visible. And not your logo – *you*.

2. Make any profile you create easy to skim. Most readers will give it 3 to 5 seconds. How much text can someone read in 3 to 5 seconds? Not much. Focus on high impact visuals and a few key words that share what you do and what's cool about you.

3. Other people's quotes often get a lot of likes or shares, but so many people post other people's quotes that it isn't a great way to stand out and showcase who *YOU* are. Try sharing your own quotes and the insights you have into what is happening in the news or trending online at the moment. Share some tidbits – pictures or comments – from your personal life. And, if something you read or watched really made you laugh or think, share that too. The big thing is to have fun with it, add value to people who will see your posts, and don't regurgitate someone else's quote just because you feel you have to post something because it's been a week since your last post.

4. Pause before posting. Before you put something online, ask yourself if you would be okay if *anyone* saw it. In other words – if someone were to take your post and put it on the front page of every major newspaper in the country, are you going to be comfortable with the message you are about to put out there?

5. Be focused and purposeful. I took the Facebook app off my phone because I found myself falling into the 'abyss' of other people's status updates far too often. I recommend that you set a *timer* before you start using any platform you're going to focus on. Set it for 15 minutes. Post something cool, useful or interesting, and then interact with a couple of people. When the timer goes off – quit.

Most importantly – know that your brand won't fail if you're not on top of social media all the time. There's always going to be a new app or a new site. You could drive yourself crazy if you try to keep up – unless that's really what you want to do.

The Last Words on Social Media

Most people are online to solve a problem or to be entertained.

Take a second right now to think about the things that you have commented on recently. What were they?

Generally people will be moved to comment on something that is funny or emotional. Something great happens – I'll cheer for you. Something sad happens – I'll send you condolences. If you make me smile or laugh, I'll probably acknowledge it with a like or a smiley emoticon.

Few people will *share* your post with others unless it's really funny, really moving or massively useful. Also, if you *ask* people to share it, they are more likely to do it. Generally, though, they want to look good in the eyes of their friends with anything they post, so your post has to make them look good for sharing.

When you are about to post something on social media, consider if this is something that would catch the attention of your ideal person. Is it something they will care about, or find funny, interesting or useful? Is it in alignment with the words you want associated with your brand?

Again, there are many platforms; try to find *one* that you like and that you'll use to give your brand a boost.

ADVERTISING ISN'T DEAD

Marketing your brand into the future, it's important to know that we're not consuming traditional marketing like we used to. The best promotions are going to be embedded in or surrounded by high value content that is targeted to the right people. Ideally your content will entertain it's target audience.

You have to be smart about the content you create, the channel you distribute it on, and the messages you put in front of your audience. But that is not to say there is no value in spending a little money on marketing and advertising.

Online ads can provide you quick and low cost results, feedback and information. There are good reasons to put some money towards online marketing even when you're first starting to build your brand.

Here are some reasons to spend money online:

1. **To Build Your Community of Subscribers**

   Once you know you have an offer that is converting – you may want to scale it up by running some ads. You'll want to consider how much you are willing to spend per person that signs up (the metric in the reports you'll get is 'cost per conversion').

   If you're new, and you don't know your business model well enough, you're probably better off not to spend much money here and to just focus on getting your content and yourself in front of other people's audiences that are a fit for your message. You can spend a lot of money and get nowhere with online ads if you don't know what you are doing or if you don't have a solid business model in place.

2. **To Test Something**

   When I wrote my first book, *More than Cashflow*, I wanted to choose a book cover that was going to stand out in a sea of tiny book icons on Amazon. I asked friends, family and clients for their opinions. From there, I created Facebook ads to test which of the favorite two covers got clicked on the most. Interestingly, it was not the cover that most people preferred when I asked for their opinions, but I went with the winner of the online test and I think it was a good choice. Almost three years later, the cheques are still rolling in every month as the book continues to sell. And, more than 80% of the sales are from online sites like Amazon where the thumbnail would matter the most.

   You can use an ad to test offers, titles, slogans and images. For a few hundred bucks you can gather some great information to help you make important decisions.

3. **To Promote an Event or Sell Your Product**

   Smartly crafted direct response marketing ads can work to fill seats or boost your sales. I had the pleasure of sitting beside two guys from the DollarBeardClub.com at a Facebook Ad training event in 2016. Their company is a great example of delivering entertainment value in one's ads while also making an immediate offer to viewers/readers to purchase a trial membership in their club. And their model is working; their company is growing rapidly.

If you aren't sure what direct response marketing is, you're probably not quite ready to spend money online. You will definitely want to study it before you put your pennies into ads, or those pennies will quickly turn into large dollar donations to Facebook or Google as you send them money without getting results.

Essentially, your goal with a direct response ad is to get the person reading the ad to take a specific action – click, subscribe, buy or call, for example.

Start with a small budget and expand it if the offer is working. You can also use retargeting to capture people who visit your site but don't take action right away. (Google it if you want to understand it technically.) Here's a real world example to help you understand the application of it: I've begun to shop online for a GPS running watch. By clicking an ad for a particular watch, I'm now being followed by the watch everywhere I go online. I see it on Facebook, on the side of my Yahoo mail, and on a few other websites. Because I visited the watch website, a tracking pixel has me tagged as a potential watch buyer and the watch company has paid for ads.

Your potential client might not want to start their diet today, but they know they will want to get going before their daughter's wedding or after their holiday, so they might sign up for your offer of a 'How to Eat Treats and Stay Fit Over the Holidays' guide *now*, and then be receptive to another one of your offers in six weeks. Facebook will even let you market directly to people who just got home from a vacation (a little creepy, I know, but as a marketer this could be incredibly useful). Or, you can put the tracking pixel on your website and post an ad in a few weeks to try to connect with them again. Both ways work and both are effective uses of online advertising.

Focus on having a clear call to action for your search ad. Generally, the best money is spent to build a relationship, not to get likes or followers.

Marketing is not dead; it's just evolving along with how we consume content. Building a successful brand is not about being on every social media site or even any one site in particular. It's about using whatever methods work for you to create a relationship, add value, and have fun with your ideal people.

 KEY ACTION ITEMS:

- Check your website (if you have one). Does it tell your customer what you do for them, or does it brag about how great you are? If you have sales copy, is it all about you, or is it about your client?

- Download a content calendar example at thenewbrandyou.com and start planning the content you'll create to add value to your audience.

- Focus your time on creating great content, meeting people who can help you grow your audience, and engaging with the people that do find their way to you. And don't focus on comparing yourself to the one-sided views of their lives that are posted online.

- Tips to maximize your social media time: Have a great close-up profile picture of yourself on your profile pages; write creative and cool profiles that are easy to skim; focus on adding value; pause before posting anything to make sure it's in alignment with your brand; and be focused and purposeful.

CHAPTER 18

Permission To Create Your Personal Brand

You remember 2008 right? It was ugly! Buying a home became next to impossible for many people as banks changed their mortgage lending rules, millions of Americans walked from their homes, and Lehman Brothers collapsed – leaving stock holders with nothing and 25,000 people without jobs.

So, naturally, it was a *perfect* time to build two businesses ... in *real estate*.

I had convinced myself that I was passionate about real estate. But really, it was just that when I realized I couldn't work for someone else anymore, real estate was right in front of me. It was what I knew, so it made sense for us to focus on growing our portfolio and building a training company to help others make better decisions around their property investments. If the mortgage crisis gave me anything, it was proof that people needed better advice to help them make their investment decisions.

It would have been tough to leave my cushy six-figure salary to build real estate businesses at *any* time, but trying to navigate the crazy waters of the aftermath of 2008 made the challenges even more enormous. But my husband and I did what we had to do, worked long hours, invested what little money we were making into our businesses instead of spending it on a lot of the fun things our friends were doing, and we built the businesses.

We went from sweating it out contacting close to 100 people to raise $300,000 for a rental house in 2009, to buying a $3.1 million medical office building after making four phone calls and having one face-to-face meeting. In 2010, I was pitching a dozen blogs, media outlets, and other online marketers *every* month with the goal of getting featured to their audiences. In February 2016, Entrepreneur.com – one of the top 1000 websites in the world – did a feature on us out of nowhere. I didn't even contact them or know the author of the article.

What was the difference? Really, it came down to one thing. We worked incredibly hard – harder than many people would want to work – but a big part of the intense efforts went into building a *brand* that people knew about and could trust.

I always took action and tried everything I learned … but no matter what technique we uncovered or what strategy we tried, we always found selling and convincing people to work with us was nerve wracking and uncomfortable. When we *refocused* on becoming the known authority and attracting the right people – that's when things finally got easier.

I soon realized it all came back to the *image* you create in the minds of the people you interact with – no matter where that interaction takes place (online or offline). Even when you're not speaking, you're communicating a strong message, and if you haven't carefully considered who you are and how you help others, and tried to showcase that, a lot is left to chance.

And, when things are left to chance, there's a high probability you will struggle and not understand why it's such a struggle.

In business, you constantly have to sell yourself – so you always have to do the work. Why not make it easier for yourself in the future by working just a little harder *now* to become the name that people trust?

After reading this book, you have all kinds of ideas and action items to help you carefully consider who you are and how you're going to showcase your personality, expertise and values to attract some fabulous folks to work with you. The question is, will you dive in and do the work?

THE ANGELINA EFFECT

If money is not your primary motivator, then the fact that your brand will boost your income may not be the message you need to hear. But, if money isn't what gets you out of bed in the morning (I like money, but it's not my first priority either), then you're probably looking for a way to have a bigger *impact*. Maybe you want to be home for your children, or maybe you want to help people in your community, or maybe you want to reach a larger audience. Possibly you have a story you know people need to hear so they can make better choices in their life.

You can achieve whatever you want if you build a great personal brand and become a name people know, trust and respect. When you do that, you'll find that your calls get through to the right people. When you want to talk about an important issue, you have an audience that will listen. And when you need to rally people to action, your voice will be powerful and it will be heard.

Angelina Jolie is an interesting example of someone with a powerful brand who uses it to have an impact. To me her personal brand is one of beauty, compassion, and purpose, all with an edge.

In 2013, Time magazine featured her on the cover with an article titled *The Angelina Effect*. It followed the aftermath of her decision not just to have, but to publicly discuss, her double mastectomy as cancer prevention. She opened up the discussion about the options for women to help *prevent* cancer ... not just to fight it when you get it.

Her openness caused huge debate over her decisions. But her goal was to create awareness so as to empower women and she achieved that.

Many women have made the same decision; but without a strong brand, a public declaration of one's choice won't make ripples, let alone waves. Her brand and her celebrity status give her the potential to impact people all over the world.

She believes in fighting for people who don't have a voice to fight for themselves. Her name gives her the ability to speak for those that wouldn't be heard otherwise.

Her brand began as an actor. She was known, but she didn't become famous until she played Lara Croft, a role that captured audiences all over the world as she played a sexy, bad ass, powerful woman.

That role, filmed largely in Cambodia, also introduced her to the troubles of war torn countries. She began to use her name to connect with people at the UN and organizations all over the world that do work in conflict-stricken areas.

She kept acting, of course, but today she is just as well known and awarded for her humanitarian efforts as she is for acting.

With her international reputation, she is now writing and directing films and expanding her career to do the projects that most interest and appeal to her.

You don't need to be one of the most famous women in the world to have an impact, but hopefully you do see how having a name people know can open your life to many possibilities to make a powerful impact and to create income.

THE RACE TO BUILD YOUR BRAND

As you finish reading this book, I hope you are excited about the possibilities of becoming a name that people recognize. If you've been taking action as you complete each chapter, you may already be seeing the results and the opportunities.

But I want you to know something. This is just the start. And starting is pretty easy. It's exciting; you have energy; and hopefully you have support from your friends and family. But there will be tough times. I want you to know this now so you can expect it and prepare to keep going.

Watch for the pesky middle.

It's like running a race.

Before the race begins, you feel excited. There's music. People are energized. The air is fresh and cool. Your legs feel ready ... almost twitchy like they can't wait to get going.

You line up, take a deep breath, and the gun goes off! Your legs feel so light as you sprint out with the rest of the runners. It feels amazing.

About five minutes into the race, it's getting tougher to breathe. You keep going, knowing that it's normal to feel that preliminary bit of fatigue.

Ten minutes in, you round the corner to see a long uphill section. Your legs are getting heavy. You think "maybe I should walk the hill ... save my energy for later," but you're not even half way yet, so you decide to push yourself up that hill.

You take a deep breath, swing your arms a little harder, and power your legs up the hill. Suddenly you're gasping for air. *"This sucks,"* you say to yourself out loud. Your legs feel like dead weight. You want to walk so badly. You glance to the side, wondering if you can cut into the alley and skip a few kilometers.

You look around and see a few people walking. And you notice one guy stepping off to the side and sitting down. *"Yeah – you have the right idea. This is so hard!"* you think as you plod past them.

You aren't sure how much further it is to the finish because you can't see it. You don't think you're even half way. *"What's the point? Do I even care if I finish?"* you ask yourself.

This is the critical point in your race and in your business. You will question yourself. You will think of all kinds of 'rational' reasons why you really don't need to finish the race, and why it may not be important to work on standing out and having an impact.

This is the pesky middle.

You'll start to think things like: 'You know, business is okay right now, I don't need to keep pushing to find new audiences to get in front of.'

Or 'maybe I should take that job offer – this might not work out and I have to support my family.'

It *will* get hard. Every time you start a new project, you'll find distractions; you'll look for an easier way; and you'll consider quitting, probably more than once. And your reasons for quitting will sound very rational.

If you can find it in your heart and mind to keep going, just focusing on the next step and then the next step, you'll soon look up to find you're now more than 20 minutes into the run and you see a sign that says *1.5km left.*

It still sucks ... no doubt about that. You feel so tired and it's so hard to keep going, but it's just a little bit easier now that you know how much further you have to go.

You come around a corner and you can hear cheers, music and the race announcer calling people's names as they cross the finish line. Suddenly you feel a jolt of energy hit your body – you're almost done – and with relief and excitement you sprint across the finish line.

As you head straight to the refueling station, you smile with pride. "*Yes! I am done!*" and after you eat half a bagel and an orange slice, you think, "*That was actually kind of fun. I wonder when the next one is*".

Business is a lot like that.

Every time you start something new, you experience those kinds of feelings.

When you start to see the results from your effort to build your brand, you'll be energized. When sales come in without effort, or opportunities find their way to you when you are least expecting them, it will be like you're at the refueling station.

Your challenge is getting through the pesky middle.

In real life, that pesky middle doesn't take minutes; it can take months, even years. The great news is that building your *brand* gives you a rock solid foundation to build from. With a solid foundation, you can build whatever you want. Your brand will carry you through and make getting through the middle of anything much easier!

You see ... once you've run one race, you know you can do another. Once you have a good brand, you can build on it. You just keep building your belief in yourself.

If you want to do the thing that is burning inside of you ... you're going to have to do the work. But the work you do today will make everything you do in the future much easier.

TURNING THE LIGHT ON IN THAT DARK ROOM

It was more than five years ago that I was facing the whiteboard with a marker in my hand trying to *draw* what else could be possible for my life.

It's hard to really describe how terrifying it was to poke my head into *that dark room* and begin to face the fact that I had left one job I didn't want to do, only to work intensely hard to grow two businesses that I *now* didn't want to do anymore.

However, I then saw the light! I realized that the effort, energy and investment that went into building my brand as Julie Broad was not wasted just because I was no longer under the real estate banner. *The hard work does* not *go to waste; it lays the foundation for the next chapter.*

I know you're probably tired of me saying this, and I am also fully aware that it does sound a bit corny, but '*You are your brand!*'

When your brand is *you* – when it's your personality, your values and what you love to do – **you can create your future. Your future is in your hands.**

Someone who trusted me as their real estate coach doesn't stop trusting me just because I have shifted the topics that I focus on and talk about. They still trust me to have their best interests at heart, give them thoughtful guidance, and give them a caring but firm push when they need it. Or maybe we no longer work together, but they will refer their friends and family and colleagues to me, because of who I am.

The brand is *me* ... and that brand doesn't change just because my focus and expertise has shifted.

Maybe you're staring at your very own ***dark room*** right in front of you. The door to the room is wide open – inviting you to find the courage to step inside and see what awaits you.

It's scary. Even if you have already begun to step inside the room, you're probably still feeling fearful of what lies further inside. Maybe you're worried about not being up for the challenge... and what if it doesn't work out?

I want you to know that even if it *does* work out, you may still want to change and do something else in five years. And, that's okay. Because if you work to add value to the lives of everyone you encounter, and become known for being a person of value who can be trusted – the work you do becomes the foundation for your future. It's not wasted.

It took me two years before I even put one foot in that room, and another year before I fully jumped inside to look around. But, I'm *so* glad I did. There are so many cool opportunities and possibilities in this room. And it feels like home. I still need to decorate more and really settle in, but I feel comfortable here ... like this is where I belong right now.

The future is exciting again! We just hung up the phone with a US immigration lawyer. As you read this, we might be living in Los Angeles, or planning our move down there.

If I had never started to look inside that dark room, it's quite likely my husband may never have come to terms with what he'd always wanted to do either – be an actor. And whatever the future may hold, at least he'll never look back and wonder 'what if' he had pursued his dream of becoming an actor?

BE YOU – YOU'RE THE ONLY PERSON WORTH BEING

So many books, courses, and consultants will tell you 'this is the way to build your brand.'

But there really are no rules. There is no 'one way' to do it.

If you take one message from these pages, I hope it's that there is only one thing you *must* do to succeed in creating a great brand – and that is **be your unique self!** That's when the magic happens.

Whatever you want to do in life, the missing piece is **always** action. Now that you've read this book, think about the steps and tips that resonated with you the most, and get to work.

Oh. One last thing - before you rush out the door excited to build your brand, take a quick look down. Are you wearing pants?

Bibliography

Anderson, Rindy C., & Casey A. Klofstad., *Preference for Leaders with Masculine Voices Holds in the Case of Feminine Leadership Roles*. December 12, 2012. http://dx.doi.org/10.1371/journal.pone.0051216

Baum, Charles L., & William F. Ford. "The wage effects of obesity: a longitudinal study," *Health Economics* Vol. 13, Issue 9, Feb. 2004, p. 24.

Berger, Jonah. *Contagious: Why Things Catch On*. Toronto: Simon & Schuster, 2013.

Cardone, Grant. *The 10x Rule: The Only Difference Between Success and Failure*. Hoboken, New Jersey: John Wiley & Sons Inc., 2011.

Carter, Judy. *The Comedy Bible*. New York: Fireside, 2001.

Christakis, Nicholas A., & James H. Fowler. *Connected: How Your Friends' Friends' Friends Affect Everything You Feel, Think, and Do*. New York: Back Bay Books, 2011.

Cialdini, Robert B. *Influence: The Psychology of Persuasion*. New York: Collins, 2007.

Clark, Dorie. *Stand Out – How to Find Your Breakthrough Idea and Build a Following Around It*. New York: Penguin, 2015.

Coleman, Daniel. *Emotional Intelligence: Why It Can Matter More than I.Q.* New York: Bantam Dell, 1995.

Collins, Jim. *Good to Great*. New York: Harper Collins Publishers, 2001.

Donovan, Jeremey. *How to Deliver a TED Talk: Secrets of the World's Most Inspiring Presentations.* 2012.

Gitomer, Jeffrey. *21.5 Unbreakable Laws of Selling.* New York: Bard Press, 2013.

Harris, Peter. *How Many Jobs Do Canadians Hold in a Lifetime.* Dec. 4, 2014.

http://careers.workopolis.com/advice/
how-many-jobs-do-canadians-hold-in-a-lifetime/

Helitzer, Mel. *Comedy Writing Secrets.* New York: Writers Digest Books, 2005.

Hill, Napoleon. *Think and Grow Rich.* Meriden, Connecticut: The Ralston Society, 1938.

Jones, Steve. *Start You Up: Rock Star Secrets to Unleash Your Personal Brand and Set Your Career on Fire.* Austin: Greenleaf Book Group Press, 2014.

Kenney, Dan S. and Matt Zagula. *No B.S. Trust-Based Marketing: The Ultimate Guide to Creating Trust in an Understandably Untrusting World.* Irvine, CA: Entrepreneur Press, 2012.

Kiyosaki, Robert with Sharon L. Lechter. *Rich Dad Poor Dad*, New York: Warner Books, 1997.

Klaff, Oren. *Pitch Anything.* Toronto: McGraw Hill, 2011.

Lekushoff, Andrea. "Lifestyle-driven virtual teams: A new paradigm for professional services firms." *Ivey Business Journal,* Sept./Oct. 2012.

http://iveybusinessjournal.com/publication/lifestyle-driven-virtual-teams-a-new-paradigm-for-professional-services-firms/

Losier, Michael. *The Law of Attraction: The Science of Attracting More of What You Want and Less of What You Don't.* Toronto: Grand Central Life & Style, 2010.

McKee, Robert. *Story: Substance, Structure, Style, and the Principles of Screenwriting.* New York: Harper Collins, 1997.

Milgram, Stanley. *Obedience to Authority: The Experiment that Challenged Human Nature.* New York: Harper Perennial, 2009

Murphy, Mark. *Hard Goals.* Toronto: McGraw Hill, 2011.

Ogilivy, David. *Ogilivy on Advertising.* New York: Vintage Division of Random House, 1983.

Pressfield, Steven. *The War of Art: Break Through the Blocks and Win Your Inner Creative Battles.* New York: Black Irish Entertainment LLC, 2002.

Roehling, Mark V. "Weight based discrimination in employment: psychological and legal aspects." Department of Management, Western Michigan University. *Personnel Psychology*, 11/1999, 52(4): 969-1016.

Simmons, Annette. *The Story Factor: Secrets of Influence from the Art of Storytelling.* New York: Basic Books, 2006.

Solnick, Sara J. and Maurice E. Schweitzer. "The influence of physical attractiveness and gender on ultimatum game decisions." *Organizational Behavior and Human Decision Processes.* Vol. 79, No. 3, Sept. 1999. p. 199–215.

Article ID obhd.1999.2843, available online at http://www.idealibrary.com on

Warren, Blair. *Forbidden Keys to Persuasion* (An online course that is no longer available.) www.blairwarren.com

Acknowledgments

I've seen people promoting programs that promise to turn you into a published author in just three months. Considering that this book took me over a year to research and write, and that it was in the editing phase for over four months, the thought that someone can help you research, write, edit and publish a book worth reading in three months seems a bit unrealistic to me. But I guess if you have an outstanding team of people dedicated to your project, anything is possible. Personally, I know that this book would not have been possible without some amazing people helping me along the way....

To my content editors, Scott Sylvan Bell, Rhonda Branson, Dave Peniuk and Zander Robertson, who read the early drafts of this book, thank you for your encouragement and enthusiasm, and for the many ideas that helped enhance the value of this book in so many ways – thank you so much!

To my copy editor, Cathy Reed, I send a huge hug of appreciation because the book went from something I thought was okay to something I am proud of, thanks to all of your thoughtful suggestions and careful edits.

To Philip McKernan, I want to say thank you for always having my back and for challenging me to look at what else is possible for my life. This book wouldn't exist without you.

To Kevin Hogan, thank you for your support and ideas throughout the creation of this book, and beyond that, for all you've done to help and guide me. I also want to let you – and anyone reading this book – know that, while I tried to *source* every idea or concept that I learned from *you*, the truth is I have benefitted so much from your knowledge and wisdom in the last five years that I'm sure I have unintentionally presented some things as *my* ideas when they actually originated from *you*. Thankfully, besides being brilliant and having so many ideas worth borrowing, you have always been generous and supportive – so I hope you will forgive me for any such oversights.

Thank you also to my Mom, Ruth-Anne Broad, for her final review of the manuscript. I know you wanted me to include more 'Julie stories', but some stories are ones only a devoted and supportive Mom like you would love to read. Thank you to my husband Dave Peniuk for his never ending support as I rode the emotional roller coaster of writing another book and continuing my journey as an entrepreneur. And, finally, to *all* my friends, family and clients … thank you. Without your support there would be nobody to read my writing or watch my videos. I hope this book and my work add value to your life and business in some way, but please know that just by reading, watching and sharing with others you are helping me to do something I love to do and that means a lot to me – THANK YOU!

56360068R00162

Made in the USA
Charleston, SC
19 May 2016